对外汉语本科系列教材

语言技能类　　一年级教材

# 汉语口语教程
## HANYU KOUYU JIAOCHENG
### 第二册

杨寄洲　贾永芬　编著

北京语言大学出版社
BEIJING LANGUAGE AND CULTURE
UNIVERSITY PRESS

© 2022 北京语言大学出版社，社图号 22119

图书在版编目（CIP）数据

汉语口语教程. 第二册 ／ 杨寄洲，贾永芬编著. --
北京：北京语言大学出版社，2022.12（2025.2 重印）
　ISBN 978-7-5619-6176-6

　Ⅰ.①汉… Ⅱ.①杨… ②贾… Ⅲ.①汉语－口语－
对外汉语教学－教材 Ⅳ.① H195.4

中国版本图书馆 CIP 数据核字（2022）第 197787 号

## 汉语口语教程 第二册
### HANYU KOUYU JIAOCHENG DI-ER CE

| | |
|---|---|
| 责任编辑： | 王巧燕　赫　栗 |
| 排版制作： | 北京创艺涵文化发展有限公司 |
| 责任印制： | 周　燚 |

| | |
|---|---|
| 出版发行： | 北京语言大学出版社 |
| 社　　址： | 北京市海淀区学院路 15 号，100083 |
| 网　　址： | www.blcup.com |
| 电子信箱： | service@blcup.com |
| 电　　话： | 编辑部　8610-82303647/3592/3724 |
| | 国内发行　8610-82303650/3591/3648 |
| | 海外发行　8610-82303365/3080/3668 |
| | 北语书店　8610-82303653 |
| | 网购咨询　8610-82303908 |
| 印　　刷： | 北京富资园科技发展有限公司 |

| | | | |
|---|---|---|---|
| 版　次： | 2022 年 12 月第 1 版 | 印　次： | 2025 年 2 月第 3 次印刷 |
| 开　本： | 787 毫米 × 1092 毫米　1/16 | 印　张： | 12.25 |
| 字　数： | 210 千字 | | |
| 定　价： | 55.00 元 | | |

PRINTED IN CHINA

凡有印装质量问题，本社负责调换。QQ：1367565611，电话：010-82303590

# 前 言

《汉语口语教程》是为零起点的汉语学习者编写的口语教材，适用于开展学历教育和非学历教育以及各类国际汉语教育的教学单位。

**本教程的编写理念是：力求培养学生成才。**

选择学习汉语的外国学生，尤其是来华学习汉语的留学生大多处于人生的最佳年龄段，他们万里迢迢来到中国，来到我们身边，追求自己的人生梦想，跟我们学习汉语，我们不能辜负了他们。我们一定要树立培养学生成才的理念，哪怕学生只学一年半载，也要为他们今后的发展着想。

**口语课是单项技能训练课。**

如果说听力课和阅读课重在输入的话，那么口语课则重在输出。这就要求学生在课堂上要尽可能多地开口说话，要求教师要借助教材，调动和利用一切教学手段和技巧，激发学生的表达欲望。师生之间、生生之间要开展接近实际的交际会话，培养、操练学生的口头表达能力。要让学生通过一年的学习，能够运用汉语满足日常交际需要，并为他们升入高年级或进入其他专业学习（如学医、学工等）打下一个良好的基础。

**口语课堂应是师生互动、演示教材的"剧场"。**

我们希望，任课教师一定要充分利用课堂，充分利用师生面对面的语境，指导并共同进行师生之间、生生之间的交际会话。课堂交际会话当然是模拟实际生活的会话，尽管如此，这四五十分钟的一节课，对于学生来说都弥足珍贵。我们建议教师不要过多地使用PPT，您面对学生真诚坦然的微笑，亲切悦耳的话语，声情并茂的讲解与朗读，与学生面对面、心与心的交流，这是任何教材、任何课件都无法代替的。

口语课堂上，教师和学生都要动起来。再好的教材都是死的。语言是交际的工具，是最灵动、最活泼、最实用的。尤其是初级阶段，学生能不能尽快用汉语进行最实用的交际，对他们的影响巨大而深远。

口语应是带表情的动与说的结合。所以建议教师活用教材，把课堂当成"剧场"，把教材当成"剧本"，教师当好导演，学生当好演员，师生互动，把每节课都演成一幕话剧。

本教程分4册共64课，供零起点的汉语学习者使用1年。4册书共出生词约2000个，多为常用词。

鉴于各个教学单位口语课的课时不统一，有多有少，所以，完全可以从本单位的实际出发，从教学对象的实际出发，灵活使用本教程。

**编写体例**

一、课文

本教程的课文多是情景会话。情景设计都基于来华留学生的学习和生活。编者的意图是，学习和练习这些会话，使学习者能熟练地运用它们，满足日常学习和生活的交际需要。

为了尽早培养学生的成段表达能力，本教程从第一册第10课起，就设置了一个"读后说"的练习项目。其内容都是一些小短文。

课文是重中之重！

课堂上教师要集中精力，用大量时间带领学生把课文读熟。教师要大声示范朗读，大声领读；同时，要求学生大声跟读、大声齐读、大声地单独朗读。

朗读是口语课堂教学和课外练习的主要方法。要鼓励学生大声地、反复地朗读，让学生通过朗读感受汉语的语音语调和语气，领略汉语的语言美。不论是会话课文还是叙述短文，都要求学生最少要朗读十遍以上，达到熟读成诵的程度。这样，也只有这样，用的时候才能脱口而出。

通过一年的训练，大多数学生的口语能力应能基本满足日常学习和生活的交际需要。这是被多年教学实践证明了的。

第一、二册（1～32课）的课文都配有汉语拼音，同时提供英文译文供学生参考。拼音是为了减少学生朗读的困难，英文译文是为了减少学生理解的困难。我们的教学对象大多具有高中以上学历，尽管英语不一定是每个学生的母语，但本教程的内容都是基础的日常会话，英文译文对他们理解课文应该有所帮助。

第三、四册（33～64课）除了生词加注拼音和英文释义外，课文不再加注拼音，也不再提供英文译文。

效果如何，要由教学实践来检验。我们希望听到一线教师的意见和建议，以便及时修正。

二、生词

本教程每课的生词部分都有拼音、词性和英文释义。

三、注释

口语课堂教学没有讲练语法的任务，因此，本教程的注释只是对课文中出现的一些语法点或重点词语的用法加以简要的说明，为教师教学提供一些方便。例句可供学习者参考。

四、练习

口语课重在培养学生"说"的言语技能，但听说读写这四项言语技能既相对独立又相互依存，既相互制约又相互促进。听不懂，一定不会说；读不懂，也一定影响说。没有大量的输入，就不可能有理想的输出。因此，口语课要达到预期的效果，必须充分利用各项言语技能的相互促进作用，通过有效的输入，激发表达欲望，促进齿舌运动，使学习者发出正确的汉语语音语调，说出正确的有交际意义的句子，从而达到日常学习和生活想要达到的交际目的。

本教程通用的练习是：朗读并分辨近音字词的语音语调、替换、选词填空、完成句子或会话并大声朗读、结合自身实际回答问题等。

口语课必须重视语音语调的训练。因此，本教程始终把语音语调的练习放在非常重要的位置。教材在这方面的努力，也是为教学做个提示：要想让学生说一口正确的汉语普通话，教师的作用是教材无法代替的。

练习要求学生课外完成，教师可及时检查和纠正，以提高学生的学习质量。

练习不仅是复练课堂所学，同时希望学生能够通过做练习，培养自学能力。严格地说，没有自学能力的学生不可能成才。在网络时代，只要想学、爱学，随时都可以学习。要引导学生刻苦自学、努力成才。所以，本教程在练习中一再提示，遇到不懂的词语、不懂的文化知识点，要去问百度、问谷歌，要随手去查电子词典——它们都是课外的"老师"。教师要鼓励学生自学，帮助学生培养良好的学习习惯。

在初级阶段，受词汇、语法的制约，会话课文都是情景会话。情景会话就必然受情景的限定。为了弥补初级口语会话的不足，我们在每课练习部分的最后，添加了一个"怎么表达"，这实际就是交际会话。一般说来，交际会话的句子和会话不太受情景的制约。需要说明的是，这也不属于课堂教学的内容，而是为学生自学准备的。

练习中的诗词和著名词句都是学生自学的内容。出诗词的目的是想利用其合辙押韵的特点，培养学生的朗读兴趣，同时也为他们今后的深造奠定基础。一些我们耳熟能详的词句，让学生接触一下，不无益处。

本教程的编写得到业内朋友的指导和帮助，北京语言大学出版社也给予大力支持，在此表示衷心的感谢。

编者
2022年6月

# Preface

*Spoken Chinese Course* is written for Chinese beginners. It is suitable for the academic institutions developing credential and non-credential education, as well as teaching Chinese to speakers of other languages.

**The compiling idea of this course is to strive to cultivate students' talents.**

The foreign students who choose to study Chinese, especially those who come to China to study Chinese, are at their best ages in life. They come all the way to China, to us, to pursue their dreams of life and learn Chinese with us, thus we can't let them down. We must hold the belief to cultivate students' talents. Even if they just study for a year or so, we should consider their future development.

**The oral class is a single-skill training course.**

While the listening and reading classes focus on input, the oral class stresses output. Therefore, students are required to speak as much as possible in class, and teachers are required to stimulate students' desire to express themselves adopting all kinds of teaching methods and techniques by the aid of the coursebook. Genuine conversations should take place between the teacher and students, as well as among students, in order to develop and train students' oral expression ability. After one year's study, students should be able to have daily communication in Chinese, and lay a solid foundation for their further study in higher grades or other majors (e.g. medicine, engineering, etc.).

**The oral class should be a theater for the teacher to interact with students and demonstrate the coursebook.**

We hope that the teacher can make full use of the class and the face-to-face context between him/her and students to guide and make teacher-student and student-student conversations. Classroom conversation is of course a conversation that stimulates real life. Nevertheless, the 40- to 50-minute lesson is especially valuable for students. We suggest teachers try not to use PPT too much. Your sincere and calm smile, kind and sweet words, remarkable explanation and reading aloud, and your face-to-face and heart-to-heart communication with students cannot be replaced by any coursebook or courseware.

In the oral class, both the teacher and students should be active. No matter how good the coursebook is, it is rigid. Language is the tool of communication. It is the most intelligent, active and practical. Especially in the primary stage, whether students can use Chinese to communicate as soon as possible has a huge and far-reaching impact on them.

Spoken language should be a combination of expressive movement and speech. So teachers are advised to make flexible use of the coursebook. Teachers should take the classroom as a theater and the coursebook as the playscript. The teacher should act as the director, while students should act as actors and actresses. They should interact with each other to put on a play in each class.

This course contains four books with 64 lessons. It is suitable for Chinese beginners and can be used for one year. There are about 2,000 new words in the four books, most of which are common words.

Since the hours for the oral class vary in each institution, you can use this coursebook flexibly according to the actual conditions of your institution and your students.

**Compiling style:**

I. Texts

The texts in this coursebook are mostly situation conversations. The situations are based on the study and life of foreign students in China. The compilers aim to make students learn and practice these conversations so as to use them proficiently and meet their communicative needs in study and life.

In order to develop students' ability to express themselves in paragraph as early as possible, a "speaking after reading" part is designed from Lesson 10 of Book 1. All the texts in this part are short essays.

Texts are the most important!

In class, the teacher should focus on texts and spend much time to lead students to read texts fluently. The teacher should model reading aloud and ask students to follow, and read aloud together and individually.

Reading aloud is the main method of oral classroom teaching and extracurricular practice. Encourage students to read aloud and repeatedly. Let students perceive the pronunciation, intonation and tones of Chinese and the beauty of Chinese by reading aloud.

Whether it is a conversation text or a narrative essay, the teacher should require students to read it aloud for at least ten times to reach the level of reciting it. In this way, and only in this way, can students blurt it out when using it.

Through one year's training, most students should be able to communicate in their daily study and life. This has been proved by years of teaching practice.

Pinyin and English translation for the texts are provided in Books 1 and 2 (Lessons 1-32). The Pinyin is added to make it easier for students to read the texts aloud, and the English translation is provided to reduce students' difficulty in understanding. Most of our students have a senior high school education or above. Although English is not necessarily every student's first language, all the content of this coursebook is basic and daily conversations, and the English translation should be helpful for them to understand the texts.

In Books 3 and 4 (Lessons 33-64), except for the Pinyin and English definition for the new words, no Pinyin and English translation for the texts are provided. The effect will be tested by the teaching practice. We hope to hear the opinions and suggestions from the teachers, so as to make timely revisions.

II. New Words

The Pinyin and English definition are provided for the new words in each lesson in the coursebook.

III. Notes

Grammar is not taught and practiced in the oral class. Therefore, the notes in this coursebook are only brief explanations of some grammatical points or key words and expressions that appear in the texts, to provide convenience for teaching. Example sentences are for students' reference.

IV. Exercises

Oral class focuses on developing students' speaking skills. However, the four language skills of listening, speaking, reading and writing are relatively independent on one hand, but dependent on each other on the other hand. If you don't understand what was said, you can't speak. If you don't understand what was written, your speaking skills will also be affected. Without a large amount of input, it is impossible to have ideal output. Therefore, to achieve the expected effect in oral class, we must make full use of the mutual promotion of various language skills. Through effective input, the desire to express is stimulated, and the tongue and teeth movements are promoted. Students are able to produce correct pronunciation and intonation of Chinese, and say the correct sentences with communicative meanings, so as to achieve the communicative purpose needed in daily study and life.

The common exercises in this coursebook include reading aloud and distinguishing the pronunciation and intonation of similar words, substitution, choosing words to fill in the blanks, completing the sentences or conversations and reading them aloud, and answering the questions according to the students' actual situations.

The training of pronunciation and intonation is very important in oral class. Therefore, this coursebook always attaches great importance to the pronunciation and intonation exercises. The effort of the coursebook in this regard is also a reminder for teaching: to make students speak Mandarin correctly, the role of teachers cannot be replaced by coursebooks.

Students are required to finish the exercises after class. Teachers can check and correct them in time to improve the quality of students' study.

The exercises are designed not only to practice what students have learned in class, but also to train students' self-study ability. Strictly speaking, students without self-study ability can't be successful. In the Internet age, as long as you want to and love to learn, you can learn at any time. Teachers should guide students to study hard independently and become successful. Therefore, the course in the exercises always suggests students to consult Baidu, Google, or electronic dictionaries when meeting unfamiliar words, expressions or cultural knowledge, for they are extracurricular "teachers". Teachers should encourage students to study by themselves and help them develop good study habits.

Restricted by vocabulary and grammar in the primary stage, all the conversational texts are situation conversations. In order to make up for the deficiency of primary oral conversations, we add a "how to express" part at the end of the exercises in each lesson. They are actually communicative conversations. Generally speaking, communicative sentences and conversations are less situational. It should be noted that this part is prepared for students to study on their own instead of being taught in class.

The well-known sayings in the exercises are for students to study on their own. The purpose is to guide students to perceive the rhymes in the poems so as to develop their interests in reading aloud and lay a foundation for their further study. It is useful for students to get an initial understanding of some poems and sentences we are familiar with.

We sincerely appreciate the guidance and help from friends in this field, as well as the strong support by Beijing Language and Culture University Press when compiling this coursebook.

The Author
June 2022

# 致学习者

亲爱的同学们：

当你拿起这本书，开始学习汉语口语的时候，你的人生便开始了新的旅程。

当你离开家乡，告别父母、兄弟、同学、朋友来到中国这个陌生国度的时候，你可能有诸多的不适应。

不过没关系。任何人初到异国他乡，都会有这种感觉的。

初来乍到，一句汉语也不会说，一个汉字也不认识，一个朋友都没有，你会感到孤单、寂寞，你会感到无助、痛苦。想家，想爸爸妈妈，想兄弟姐妹，想同学朋友，甚至会哭鼻子，恨不得马上飞回国去。

不过，你一定明白，眼前的这些困难都是暂时的，很快就会过去；过去了，你将由此踏上成才之路。

你要想到自己的未来，想到你是在学习人类最美的语言之一，也是当今世界历史最悠久、使用人数最多的语言之一——汉语！

汉语之美，美不胜收；汉字之妙，妙不可言。

要让自己冷静下来，想一想：今后的路该怎么走？

不必讳言，对于来自世界各国的学习者来说，汉语的确很难学。尽管书里说不难，但是老师心里明白，学好一种外语，对谁来说都不容易。

但"艰难困苦，玉汝于成"，"吃得苦中苦，才有甜上甜"。不经历风雨，难以见彩虹，没有人能随随便便地成功。希望你放平心态，放松心情，准备迎接各种挑战。为了你，为了你的家人，相信你一定不怕苦、不怕难，勇敢地闯过一道道难关，胜利到达成功的彼岸，实现自己美好的理想，成就自己理想的人生。

为此，根据我们几十年教外国留学生的经验，向同学们提出以下几点希望。

1. 无论如何，都应该坚持每天到教室上课

学得好的学生不一定是班上最聪明的学生，但一定是最努力的学生。希望同学们能天天和你的老师、同学见面，天天和他们一起度过这愉快美好的课堂时光。上课不仅仅是学汉语，更是为了培养自己高尚的人品和高贵的人格，使自己成为一个自律且优秀的人。

2．课后一定要认真做练习

学习外语，遇到不会、不懂的词语和句子是难免的。如今是网络时代，只要你想学，处处都能找到老师。所以我们一再强调：问百度、问谷歌、查电子词典。

要努力培养自己的自学能力。可以说，没有自学能力的人不可能成才。世界上凡是学有所成的人，都有非凡的自学能力。

老师领进门，修行在个人。

那些杰出的、优秀的人虽然都有老师，但他们最后都比自己的老师更优秀！也希望你们能踏着老师的肩膀，奋勇地攀登你们人生的高峰。

3．要预习，预习比复习更重要

要变"要我学"为"我要学"，使自己时时处于主动的地位。

我们说预习比复习更重要，就是因为预习是你在主动地学。

学习外语，一定要走在老师的前边。现在的学习条件这么好，只要你有志气、肯努力，就要在上课前，把第二天要学的课文、生词都预习预习，一遍、两遍……，或者读一读、记一记。这样，你到教室去上课，将不会再有"难"的苦恼，而会觉得是一种美妙的享受。

4．多和中国人交往

语言是交际的工具。到生活中去，到中国社会中去，社会生活永远有课堂上学不到的东西。要相信，人类的大多数都是善良的，中国人也一样。只要你不怕、不害羞，你就会明白，在家靠父母，出门靠朋友。多交朋友，一定是一件非常惬意的事。在中国人面前说汉语，不要怕说错。要多说，一次说错了，再说一次可能就说对了。要不了多久，你一定能说一口流利的汉语，你的生活也会开辟一片新的天地。

至于将来做什么，将来会怎么样，请你多读书，书会告诉你的。

这本书和教这本书的老师都是你的朋友，他们将陪伴你一路走去，走向你理想的未来。

最想说的是：我们爱你们，所以献上这本书！

编者
2021年6月初稿
2022年6月定稿

## To Students

Dear students,

When you pick up this book and begin to learn spoken Chinese, your will start a new journey in your life.

When you leave your hometown, say goodbye to your parents, siblings, classmates and friends, and come to China—an unfamiliar country, you may feel much unadapted.

But it doesn't matter. Any new arrival to an alien place will have the same feeling.

When you first arrive in China, you cannot speak a word of Chinese, nor can you recognize any Chinese characters, or have any friends. You feel lonely, helpless and miserable. You miss your parents, siblings, classmates and friends. You even want to cry. You wish you would fly home immediately.

However, you must know that these immediate difficulties are temporary and will soon be overcome. When you overcome them, you will be on the road to success.

You have to think about your future, and that you are studying one of the most beautiful human languages, as well as one of the oldest and most spoken languages in the world today—Chinese!

The beauty of Chinese is too much to absorb. The wonder of Chinese characters is beyond expression.

You should calm yourself down and think about your road in future.

There is no denying the fact that Chinese is really difficult for students from all over the world. Although it is said in the books that Chinese is not difficult, teachers know that studying a foreign language well is not easy for anyone.

However, no pains, no gains. We hope that you will be prepared for challenges in a peaceful state of mind. For you and your family, we believe you won't be afraid of the difficulties and hardships, and you will get over the hurdles bravely before reaching the dreamland of success, realizing your goals, and achieving your ideal life.

To this end, based on our decades of experience in teaching foreign students, we hope you can do as follows:

1. Persist in attending class every day in any case

Those who do well in class are not necessarily the smartest students, but surely the most hard-working ones. We hope you can meet your teachers and classmates every day and spend the happy time with them in class. By attending class, you not only learn Chinese, but also cultivate noble character and make yourself a self-disciplined and excellent person.

2. Do exercises carefully after class

When studying a foreign language, it is inevitable to encounter words and sentences that you don't know or understand. In the Internet age, teachers can be found everywhere if you want to learn something. That's why we emphasize again and again that you should consult Baidu, Google, and electronic dictionaries.

Efforts should be made to develop your self-study ability. A person without the self-study ability cannot be successful. Anyone in the world who is successful in learning has an extraordinary self-study ability.

The teacher may teach, but progress is up to the hard work of the individual.

Though those outstanding people have teachers, they become more excellent than their teachers in the end! We also hope that you can also stand on the shoulders of your teachers and climb the peak of your life bravely.

3. Pay attention to previewing, which is more important than reviewing

Change "make me study" to "I want to study", and take the initiative all the time. Previewing is more important than reviewing in that you are studying on your own initiative when you preview.

When you learn a foreign language, be sure to stay ahead of your teachers. Now the learning conditions are good. As long as you are ambitious and hard-working, you can preview, read and memorize the text and new words several times before class. In this way, when you go to class, you will feel wonderful rather than difficult.

4. Make more contact with Chinese people

Language is a tool of communication. You should experience Chinese life and society, where you can learn what you cannot learn in class. People are mostly kind, so are Chinese. As long as you are not afraid or shy, you will find that you need the support of friends when away from home. It is very pleasant to make more friends. Don't be afraid of making mistakes when speaking Chinese in front of Chinese people. Talk more. If you make a mistake at first, try again and you will probably be right. You will shortly be able to speak Chinese fluently. In addition, you will explore a new world in your life.

As to your future, read more books and you will find the answer.

Both this coursebook and the teacher who uses it in class are your friends, who will accompany you all the way to your ideal future.

What we want to say most is that we offer this book because we love you!

The Author<br>
First draft in June 2021<br>
Final version in June 2022

## 一、汉语词类简称表

| 名称 | 简称 | 英文 |
|---|---|---|
| 1. 名词 míngcí | 名 | noun |
| 2. 代词 dàicí | 代 | pronoun |
| 3. 动词 dòngcí | 动 | verb |
| 4. 助动词 zhùdòngcí | 助动 | auxiliary verb |
| 5. 形容词 xíngróngcí | 形 | adjective |
| 6. 数词 shùcí | 数 | numeral |
| 7. 量词 liàngcí | 量 | measure word |
| 8. 副词 fùcí | 副 | adverb |
| 9. 介词 jiècí | 介 | preposition |
| 10. 连词 liáncí | 连 | conjunction |
| 11. 叹词 tàncí | 叹 | interjection |
| 12. 拟声词 nǐshēngcí | 拟声 | onomatopoeia |
| 13. 助词 zhùcí | 助 | particle |
| 14. 词头 cítóu | 头 | prefix |
| 15. 词尾 cíwěi | 尾 | suffix |

## 二、汉语语法术语

1. 主语 zhǔyǔ        subject
2. 谓语 wèiyǔ        predicate
3. 宾语 bīnyǔ        object
4. 定语 dìngyǔ       attribute
5. 状语 zhuàngyǔ     adverbial
6. 补语 bǔyǔ         complement

（1）程度补语 chéngdù bǔyǔ        degree complement
　　例如：形容词＋极了
　　　　这个电影好极了。

（2）状态补语 zhuàngtài bǔyǔ　　state complement

例如：动词 + 得 + 形容词 / 动词短语

他学得好不好？他学得很好。

他跑得快不快？他跑得不快。

你写得怎么样？我写得不太好。

他高兴得跳了起来。

（3）结果补语 jiéguǒ bǔyǔ　　result complement

例如：动词 + 动词 / 形容词

我的作业做完了。

瓶子里的酒喝光了。

他把这本书翻译成了英语。

（4）趋向补语 qūxiàng bǔyǔ　　complement of direction

例如：动词 + 来 / 去 / 上 / 下 / 进 / 出 / 回 / 过 / 起 / 上来 / 下去 / 回来 / 回去 / 过来 / 过去 / 起来 / 进来 / 进去……

他从楼上下来了。

我们从这儿上去吧。

我买回来一盆花。

他从外边里带进来一只小狗。

（5）可能补语 kěnéng bǔyǔ　　complement of potentiality

例如：动词 + 得 / 不 + 结果补语 / 趋向补语

中文报你看得懂看不懂？

我现在还听不懂中文广播。

屋子太小，坐不下二十个人。

你买得太多了，我吃不了。

沙发太大，搬不进去。

太重了，我提不动。

（6）数量补语 shùliàng bǔyǔ　　complement of quantity

例如：动词 + 数量短语

他比我高五厘米。

姐姐比我大两岁。

（7）时量补语 shíliàng bǔyǔ　　complement of duration
　　例如：动词 + 时量短语
　　　　　我已经学了一年了。
　　　　　他来了快一个月了。

（8）动量补语 dòngliàng bǔyǔ　　complement of frequency
　　例如：动词 + 动量短语
　　　　　我敲了一下门，但是没有人答应。
　　　　　中国我已经来过两次了。
　　　　　我把这篇文章从头到尾仔细看了一遍，没有发现错字。
　　　　　香港我去过一回，台湾我还没有去过。

# 目录 Contents

第十七课　我们相处得很好 …………………（1）

第十八课　请大家自我介绍一下儿…………（9）

第十九课　你能告诉我怎么走吗 ……………（18）

第二十课　我想开一个活期账户 ……………（26）

第二十一课　我每天都过得很愉快 …………（33）

第二十二课　想成才就必须多读书 …………（42）

第二十三课　难怪你学得这么好 ……………（51）

第二十四课　你在做什么呢 …………………（60）

第二十五课　没有手机简直没法儿活 ………（69）

第二十六课　刚才我跑步了 …………………（78）

第二十七课　我要了一碗牛肉面 ……………（88）

第二十八课　我常去超市买东西 ……………（96）

第二十九课　我买了一本英汉词典 …………（105）

第三十课　我来了三个多月了 ………………（118）

第三十一课　我请小时工帮我收拾房间 ……（131）

I

第三十二课　今天我们从这条小路爬上去 ……（142）

词汇表 …………………………………………（155）

专名 ……………………………………………（172）

# 第十七课 Lesson 17
## Dì-shíqī kè
## 我们相处得很好
## Wǒmen xiāngchǔ de hěn hǎo
## We get along very well

## 一 课文 Text

### （一）我们相处得很好

（两个留学生在谈话）

Ānlì: Nǐ zhù nǎr? Xiào nèi háishi xiào wài?
安丽：你住哪儿？校内还是校外？

Mǎlì: Wǒ zhù xiào nèi liúxuéshēng gōngyù.
玛丽：我住校内留学生公寓。

Ānlì: Nǐ zhù duōshao hào fángjiān?
安丽：你住多少号房间？

Mǎlì: Èr mén 806 hào.
玛丽：二门806号。

Ānlì: Shì yí gè rén zhù ma?
安丽：是一个人住吗？

Mǎlì: Bú shì. Wǒ hé yí gè Rìběn tóngxué hé zhù.
玛丽：不是。我和一个日本同学合住。

Ānlì: Nǐmen xiāngchǔ de zěnmeyàng?
安丽：你们相处得怎么样？

Mǎlì: Wǒmen xiāngchǔ de hěn hǎo.
玛丽：我们相处得很好。

---

**We get along very well**

Anli: Where do you live? On or off campus?

Mary: I live in the international students' apartment on campus.

Anli: What's your room number?

Mary: I live in Room 806, Door 2.

Anli: Do you live alone?

Mary: No. I live with a Japanese classmate.

Anli: How do you get along with each other?

Mary: We get along very well.

## （二）你真是幸运

Mǎlì: Tīngshuō nǐ zài yí gè Zhōngguórén jiā li zhù?
玛丽：听说你在一个中国人家里住？

Ānlì: Shì.
安丽：是。

Mǎlì: Zěnmeyàng a?
玛丽：怎么样啊？

Ānlì: Fángdōng fūfù dōu shì dàxué tuìxiū jiàoshòu, dài wǒ xiàng duì zìjǐ de nǚ'ér yíyàng, fēicháng hǎo.
安丽：房东夫妇都是大学退休教授，待我像对自己的女儿一样，非常好。

Mǎlì: Nà nǐ zhēn shì xìngyùn.
玛丽：那你真是幸运。

Ānlì: Shì a. Yǒu kòngr de shíhou dào wǒ nàr qù wánr ba, yě rènshi rènshi nà liǎng wèi kěqīn kějìng de lǎorén.
安丽：是啊。有空儿的时候到我那儿去玩儿吧，也认识认识那两位可亲可敬的老人。

Mǎlì: Hǎo de.
玛丽：好的。

---

**You're so lucky**

Mary: I've heard you live with a Chinese family.

Anli: Yes.

Mary: How is it dong?

Anli: Very good! The landlady and her husband, both retired university professors, treat me as if I were their own daughter.

Mary: You're so lucky.

Anli: Yes. Come and play with me when you've got time, and make acquaintance of the dear and respectable old couple.

Mary: OK.

## 二 生词 New Words

| | | | | |
|---|---|---|---|---|
| 1 | 相处 | xiāngchǔ | 动 | to get along with |
| 2 | 住 | zhù | 动 | to live (somewhere) |
| 3 | 校内 | xiào nèi | | on campus |
| | 内 | nèi | 名 | inside |
| 4 | 校外 | xiào wài | | off campus |
| | 外 | wài | 名 | outside |
| 5 | 公寓 | gōngyù | 名 | apartment |
| 6 | 房间 | fángjiān | 名 | room |
| 7 | 门 | mén | 名 | door |
| 8 | 合住 | hé zhù | | to live together; to share an apartment |
| 9 | 幸运 | xìngyùn | 形 | lucky |
| 10 | 听说 | tīngshuō | 动 | to hear of; to hear about |
| 11 | 里 | li | 名 | inside |
| 12 | 房东 | fángdōng | 名 | owner of a house; landlord/landlady |
| 13 | 夫妇 | fūfù | 名 | husband and wife |
| 14 | 大学 | dàxué | 名 | university; college |
| 15 | 退休 | tuìxiū | 动 | to retire |
| 16 | 教授 | jiàoshòu | 名 | professor |
| 17 | 待 | dài | 动 | to treat; to deal with |
| 18 | 对 | duì | 动 | with regard to; concerning; to |
| 19 | 自己 | zìjǐ | 代 | oneself |
| 20 | 一样 | yíyàng | 形 | the same; alike |
| 21 | 非常 | fēicháng | 副 | very |

| 22 | 空儿 | kòngr | 名 | free time |
| 23 | 时候 | shíhou | 名 | (the duration of) time |
| 24 | 到 | dào | 动 | to come/go to |
| 25 | 玩儿 | wánr | 动 | to play |
| 26 | 位 | wèi | 量 | a polite measure word for people |
| 27 | 可亲 | kěqīn | 形 | amiable; affable; genial |
|  | 可 | kě | 动 | to be worth (doing) |
| 28 | 可敬 | kějìng | 形 | worthy of respect; respectable |
| 29 | 老人 | lǎorén | 名 | old person |

### 专名 Zhuānmíng  Proper Noun

| 安丽 | Ānlì | Anli, a German student |

## 三 注释 Notes

### (一) 怎么读数字 How to read numbers

门牌号、手机号和护照号等数字，要逐个读出。例如：

Numbers such as house numbers, mobile phone numbers and passport numbers should be read out digit by digit. For example:

门牌号：二门 806 号读 èr mén bā líng liù hào。

手机号：13546789912 读 yī (yāo) sān wǔ sì liù qī bā jiǔ jiǔ yī (yāo) èr。

护照号：G 753206 读 G qī wǔ sān èr líng liù。

### (二) 数字 "0" The number "zero"

汉语读 "líng"，汉字写作 "零（〇）"。

In Chinese, the number zero is pronounced as "líng" and written as "零（〇）".

# 第十七课 Lesson 17

## 四 练习 Exercises

（一）朗读下列发音相近的词语 Read aloud the following words and expressions with similar pronunciation

| gōngyù | gōngyú | hé zhù | hézū |
| 公寓 | 工余 | 合住 | 合租 |

| xiāngchǔ | xiǎngchū | shíhou | shìhòu |
| 相处 | 想出 | 时候 | 事后 |

| rènshi | rénshì | xìngyùn | xīngyún |
| 认识 | 人世 | 幸运 | 星云 |

（二）替换并朗读 Replace and read aloud

1. A：你住多少号房间？
   B：我住二门806号。

   一门 101 号
   三门 319 号
   五门 717 号
   六门 610 号

2. A：你是一个人住还是和别人合住？
   B：我和一个日本同学合住。

   美国　　　中国
   德国　　　意大利
   尼日利亚　泰国

（三）将 A 列与 B 列连线，组成一组对话 Match A with B to make up dialogues

| A | B |
| 你要咖啡还是要茶？ | 我去。 |
| 今天谁去，你去还是他去？ | 坐高铁去。 |
| 你上午去还是下午去？ | 我喜欢蓝的。 |
| 你坐高铁去呢，还是坐飞机去？ | 我喜欢吃面。 |
| 你喜欢吃米饭还是喜欢吃面？ | 我下午去。 |
| 你喜欢红的还是蓝的？ | 我喜欢喝咖啡。 |

· 5 ·

（四）你是A，请你向B提问 Supposing you are A, ask B questions

A：_____？（还是）
B：我住校内留学生公寓。
A：_____？
B：我住二门806号房间。
A：_____？
B：我跟一个日本女孩儿合住。
A：_____？
B：我们相处得很好。

（五）选词填空并朗读下列句子 Choose the appropriate words to fill in the blanks and read aloud the following sentences

怎么样　还是　跟　得　住　多少

1. A：你住哪儿？校内_____校外？
   B：我_____校内留学生公寓。
3. A：你住_____号房间？
   B：我住二门806号。
4. A：你一个人住还是_____别人合住？
   B：我跟一个日本同学合住。
5. A：你们相处得_____？
   B：我们相处_____很好。

真　在　可亲可敬　怎么样　一样

1. 你是不是_____一个中国人家里住？
2. A：你觉得_____啊？
   B：非常好。房东夫妇都是大学退休教授，他们待我像对自己的女儿_____。

# 第十七课 Lesson 17

3. A：那你_____是幸运。

   B：是啊。有空儿到我那儿去玩儿吧，也认识认识那两位_____的老人。

(六) 根据实际情况回答问题 Answer the questions according to the actual situations

1. 你是留学生吗？
2. 你住在哪里？
3. 你住几号房间？
4. 你一个人住还是跟同学合住？
5. 你和同屋相处得怎么样？

(七) 读后说 Read the passage and say it

今天安丽和我聊天儿，她问我住校内还是住校外，我说住留学生公寓二门806号房间，我的同屋是一个日本女孩儿。她问我们相处得怎么样，我说我们相处得很好，我们是好朋友。

安丽说，她在一个中国人家里住，房东夫妇都是大学退休教授，待她像对自己的女儿一样，非常好。安丽还让我有空儿的时候去她那儿玩儿，也认识认识那两位可亲可敬的老人。

(八) 和同学一起表演课文 Act out the text with your classmates

(九) 怎么表达 How to express

> shuōmíng
> 说明 explanation

1. Lǎozǐ hé Kǒngzǐ de sīxiǎng yǐngxiǎng Zhōngguó liǎngqiān duō nián le.
   老子和孔子的思想影响中国两千多年了。
   The ideas of Laozi and Confucius have influenced China for more than 2,000 years.

2. Yīnwèi yǒu Hànzì, cái shǐ Zhōnghuá wénmíng jǐqiān nián méiyǒu zhōngduàn.
   因为有汉字，才使中华文明几千年没有中断。
   Because of the presence of Chinese characters, Chinese civilization has not

been interrupted for thousands of years.

Xuéxí Hànyǔ, rúguǒ bú rènshi Hànzì, děngyú méi xué.
3. 学习汉语，如果不认识汉字，等于没学。

If you don't know Chinese characters, you are not really learning Chinese.

(十) 朗读中国经典诗词，请注意语音语调 Read aloud the classic Chinese poem and pay attention to the pronunciation and intonation

Chìlè Gē
敕勒歌

Chìlè Chuān, Yīn Shān xià, tiān sì qiónglú, lǒnggài sìyě.
敕勒川，阴山下，天似穹庐，笼盖四野。

Tiān cāngcāng, yě mángmáng, fēng chuī cǎo dī xiàn niú yáng.
天苍苍，野茫茫，风吹草低见牛羊。

(十一) 请欣赏下列著名的词句 Please enjoy the following famous saying

Xué, ránhòu zhī bùzú.
学，然后知不足。

Learn, then know your insufficiency.

# 第十八课 请大家自我介绍一下儿
## Lesson 18 Please introduce yourselves

## 一 课文 Text

老师：请大家都自我介绍一下儿，我们互相认识认识，好吗？

学生：好！老师，您先介绍吧！

老师：我先自我介绍一下儿。我叫王伟国，是这个大学的汉语老师，今年五十岁。我的手机号码是135****1234，微信也是这个号。很高兴能跟同学们在一起。以后你们有什么问题，可以随时跟我联系。

安丽：我来说吧。我叫安丽，是德国人。我住校外一个中国人家里。我的手机号是136****5678。

马丁：我叫马丁，我是美国人。今年20岁，住留学生公寓，我还没有女朋友。我的电话是135****0987。

山本：我叫山本幸子，日本人。我也住留学生公寓，和

# 汉语口语教程 第二册
## Spoken Chinese Course (II)

　　　　　　Mǎlì shì tóngwū, wǒmen xiāngchǔ de hěn hǎo, wǒmen shì hǎo péngyou.
　　　　　　玛丽是同屋，我们相处得很好，我们是好朋友。
　　　　　　Néng lái Zhōngguó xuéxí Hànyǔ, wǒ hěn gāoxìng. Wǒ Hànyǔ shuōde bù
　　　　　　能来中国学习汉语，我很高兴。我汉语说得不
　　　　　　hǎo, qǐng dàjiā duōduō guānzhào.
　　　　　　好，请大家多多关照。

Ālǐ: 　　Wǒ jiào Ālǐ, shì Tǎnsāngníyàrén. Wǒ xué jiāotōng, míngnián yào qù
阿里：　我叫阿里，是坦桑尼亚人。我学交通，明年要去
　　　　jiāotōng dàxué xuéxí.
　　　　交通大学学习。

Àidéhuá: 　Wǒ jiào Àidéhuá, Jiānádàrén. Wǒ xuéxí Hànyǔ yǐhòu, kěnéng zài
爱德华：　我叫爱德华，加拿大人。我学习汉语以后，可能在
　　　　　Zhōngguó gōngzuò.
　　　　　中国工作。

Lǐ Xiánzhēn: Wǒ jiào Lǐ Xiánzhēn, Hánguórén, yì nián hòu qù zhōngyī dàxué xuéxí
李贤贞：　我叫李贤贞，韩国人，一年后去中医大学学习
　　　　　zhōngyī.
　　　　　中医。

Ài Hépíng: Wǒ jiào Ài Hépíng, Kěnníyàrén. Wǒ lái zhèr xiān xué yì nián Hànyǔ,
艾和平：　我叫艾和平，肯尼亚人。我来这儿先学一年汉语，
　　　　　ránhòu qù Qīnghuá Dàxué jìsuànjī xì, xuéxí réngōng-zhìnéng. Wǒ de
　　　　　然后去清华大学计算机系，学习人工智能。我的
　　　　　lǐxiǎng shì dāng yí gè kēxuéjiā.
　　　　　理想是当一个科学家。

---

**Please introduce yourselves**

Teacher: Would you please introduce yourselves so that we can get to know each other?

Students: Good! Teacher, you first.

Teacher: OK, let me introduce myself. My name is Wang Weiguo. I am a Chinese teacher in this university. I'm fifty years old. My phone number is 135****1234, which is also my WeChat ID. I am very happy to be with you. If you have any questions in the future, please feel free to contact me.

Anli: I'll go first. My name is Anli and I'm German. I live off campus with a Chinese family. My cell phone number is 136****5678.

Martin: I'm Martin. I'm American. I am 20 years old and live in the international students' apartment. I don't have a girlfriend. My number is 135****0987.

# 第十八课 Lesson 18

Yamamoto: My name is Sachiko Yamamoto. I'm Japanese. I also live in the international students' apartment. Mary and I are roommates. We get along very well. We are good friends. I am very happy to come to China to learn Chinese. I don't speak Chinese well. I'd appreciate your help in the future.

Ali: My name is Ali and I am from Tanzania. I am here to study Transportation. I'm going to study at Jiaotong University next year.

Edward: My name is Edward. I'm from Canada. I probably will work in China after learning Chinese.

Li Xianzhen: My name is Li Xianzhen, and I am from South Korea. One year later, I will go to study Traditional Chinese Medicine.

Ai Heping: My name is Ai Heping. I'm Kenyan. I'm here to study Chinese for one year. Then I will go to the Computer Science and Technology Department of Tsinghua University to study Artificial Intelligence. My dream is to be a scientist.

## 二 生词 New Words

| 1 | 自我 | zìwǒ | 代 | self |
| 2 | 先 | xiān | 副 | first |
| 3 | 今年 | jīnnián | 名 | this year |
| 4 | 岁 | suì | 量 | year of age |
| 5 | 以后 | yǐhòu | 名 | afterwards |
| 6 | 随时 | suíshí | 副 | at any time |
| 7 | 联系 | liánxì | 动 | to contact |
| 8 | 女 | nǚ | 形 | woman; female 女护士 female nurse |
|   | 男 | nán | 形 | man; male 男/女学生 boy/girl student |
| 9 | 同屋 | tóngwū | 名 | roommate |
| 10 | 关照 | guānzhào | 动 | to look after |
| 11 | 交通 | jiāotōng | 名 | transportation |
| 12 | 明年 | míngnián | 名 | next year |
| 13 | 要 | yào | 助动 | will; be going to |

| 14 | 中医 | zhōngyī | 名 | traditional Chinese medicine |
| 15 | 然后 | ránhòu | 连 | then; afterwards; after that |
| 16 | 计算机 | jìsuànjī | 名 | computer |
| 17 | 系 | xì | 名 | department |
| 18 | 人工智能 | réngōng-zhìnéng | | Artificial Intelligence (AI) |
| | 人工 | réngōng | 形 | artificial |
| | 智能 | zhìnéng | 名 | intelligence |
| 19 | 理想 | lǐxiǎng | 名 | ideal; dream |
| 20 | 当 | dāng | 动 | to be; to work as |
| 21 | 科学家 | kēxuéjiā | 名 | scientist |
| | 科学 | kēxué | 名 | science |

## 专名 Zhuānmíng  Proper Nouns

| 1 | 王伟国 | Wáng Wěiguó | Wang Weiguo, a Chinese teacher |
| 2 | 德国 | Déguó | Germany |
| 3 | 山本幸子 | Shānběn Xìngzǐ | Sachiko Yamamoto, a Japanese student |
| 4 | 日本 | Rìběn | Japan |
| 5 | 阿里 | Ālǐ | Ali, a Tanzanian student |
| 6 | 坦桑尼亚 | Tǎnsāngníyà | Tanzania |
| 7 | 爱德华 | Àidéhuá | Edward |
| 8 | 加拿大 | Jiānádà | Canada |
| 9 | 李贤贞 | Lǐ Xiánzhēn | Li Xianzhen, a Korean student |
| 10 | 韩国 | Hánguó | South Korea |
| 11 | 艾和平 | Ài Hépíng | Ai Heping, a Kenyan student |

| 12 肯尼亚 | Kěnníyà | Kenya |
| 13 清华大学 | Qīnghuá Dàxué | Tsinghua University |

## 三 练习 Exercises

**(一) 朗读 Read aloud**

1. 朗读下列发音相近的词语 Read aloud the following words and expressions with similar pronunciation

| rènshi | rénshì | dàxué | dàxuě |
|---|---|---|---|
| 认识 | 人士 | 大学 | 大雪 |
| liánxì | liànxí | lǐxiǎng | lìxiàng |
| 联系 | 练习 | 理想 | 立项 |
| zhōngyī | zhòngyì | zhìnéng | zhǐ néng |
| 中医 | 中意 | 智能 | 只 能 |

2. 朗读下列词组 Read the following phrases aloud

| chéng fēijī | zuò gāotiě | jì kuàidì | jiào wàimài |
|---|---|---|---|
| 乘 飞机 | 坐 高铁 | 寄 快递 | 叫 外卖 |
| pāi zhàopiàn | fā wēixìn | qǔ kuàijiàn | wǎngshang jiàn |
| 拍 照片 | 发 微信 | 取 快件 | 网上 见 |

**(二) 替换并朗读 Replace and read aloud**

1. 我叫<u>马丁</u>，我是<u>美国</u>人。
   今年<u>20</u>岁。

| 玛丽 | 英国 | 26 |
| 安丽 | 德国 | 23 |
| 山本 | 日本 | 25 |

2. 我住<u>留学生公寓</u>。

一门 602 号
中国人家里
校外

3. 学汉语以后，我要在中国工作。

> 去中医大学学习中医
> 去交通大学学习交通
> 去清华大学学习人工智能

**（三）选词填空并朗读下列句子** Choose the appropriate words to fill in the blanks and read aloud the following sentences

> 一起　还　学　相处　介绍　理想　联系

1. 请大家都自我_____一下儿，我们互相认识认识，好吗？
2. 我先自我介绍一下儿。我叫王伟国，是这个大学的汉语老师。很高兴能跟同学们在_____。以后你们有什么问题，可以随时跟我_____。
3. 我叫马丁，我是美国人。今年20岁，住留学生公寓，我_____没有女朋友呢。
4. 我叫山本幸子，日本人。我也住留学生公寓，和玛丽是同屋，我们_____得很好，我们是好朋友。
5. 我叫阿里，是坦桑尼亚人，我_____交通，明年要去交通大学学习。
6. 我叫艾和平，肯尼亚人。我来这儿先学一年汉语，然后去清华大学学习人工智能，我的_____是当一个科学家。

**（四）根据实际情况回答问题** Answer the questions according to the actual situations

1. 你们班有多少个学生？
2. 他们都是哪国人？
3. 你们相处得怎么样？
4. 你们都用微信吗？
5. 你们来中国是不是只学汉语？
6. 你们以后会去哪里学习？

7. 你要学习什么？

8. 你的理想是什么？

（五）请填写下列表格，然后做自我介绍 Fill in the form below and then introduce yourself

| xìngmíng<br>姓名<br>name | |
|---|---|
| guójí<br>国籍<br>nationality | |
| niánlíng<br>年龄<br>age | |
| xìngbié<br>性别<br>gender | |
| shēngrì<br>生日<br>birthday | |
| zhuānyè<br>专业<br>major; profession | |
| lǐxiǎng<br>理想<br>ideal; dream | |
| shǒujīhào / wēixìnhào<br>手机号 / 微信号<br>cell phone number/<br>WeChat ID | |

（六）和同学一起表演课文 Act out the text with your classmates

# 汉语口语教程 第二册
# Spoken Chinese Course (II)

（七）读后说 Read the passage and say it

大家好！我先自我介绍一下儿。我叫……，是……人，今年20岁，现在在……学习汉语。我住留学生公寓一门308号。我的手机号是……。我的微信也是这个号，请同学们加我的微信，以后我们可以随时联系。来中国学习汉语，我很高兴。我也学习书法和画画儿，还打太极拳。我每天都很忙，也很快乐。

（八）怎么表达 How to express

| xúnwèn |
| 询问　inquiry |

Nǐ shì shǔ shénme de?
1. A：你是属什么的？
What year were you born in?

Wǒ shǔ yáng.
B：我属羊。
I was born in the Year of the Goat.

Nǐ de mǔyǔ shì shénme?
2. A：你的母语是什么？
What is your native language?

Wǒ shuō Yīngyǔ.
B：我说英语。
English.

Nǐ huì shuō Hànyǔ ma?
3. A：你会说汉语吗？
Can you speak Chinese?

Huì yìdiǎnr.
B：会一点儿。
I can speak a little.

(九) 朗读中国经典诗词，请注意语音语调 Read aloud the classic Chinese poem and pay attention to the pronunciation and intonation

Liáng Zhōu Cí
## 凉 州 词

[Táng] Wáng Zhīhuàn
[唐] 王 之涣（688—742）

Huáng Hé yuǎn shàng bái yún jiān, yí piàn gū chéng wàn rèn shān.
黄 河 远 上 白 云 间，一 片 孤 城 万 仞 山。

Qiāngdí héxū yuàn yángliǔ, chūnfēng bú dù Yùmén Guān.
羌笛 何须 怨 杨柳， 春风 不度 玉门 关。

(十) 请欣赏下列著名的词句 Please enjoy the following famous saying

Píng'ān shì fú.
平安 是福。

Peace is a blessing.

# 第十九课 Lesson 19
## Dì-shíjiǔ kè
## 你能告诉我怎么走吗
### Nǐ néng gàosu wǒ zěnme zǒu ma
### Can you tell me how to get there

## 一 课文 Text

（一）你能告诉我怎么走吗

A：Qǐngwèn, xuéxiào lǐbian yǒu yínháng ma?
请问，学校里边有银行吗？

B：Yǒu a.
有啊。

A：Yínháng zài nǎr?
银行在哪儿？

B：Jiù zài qiánbian.
就在前边。

A：Lí zhèr yuǎn ma?
离这儿远吗？

B：Bù yuǎn, dàgài yào zǒu wǔ fēnzhōng.
不远，大概要走五分钟。

A：Nǐ néng gàosu wǒ zěnme zǒu ma?
你能告诉我怎么走吗？

B：Nǐ cóng zhèr yìzhí wǎng qián zǒu, yínháng jiù zài mǎlù zuǒbian.
你从这儿一直往前走，银行就在马路左边。

A：Xièxie nǐ!
谢谢你！

B：Bú kèqi!
不客气！

Can you tell me how to get there

A: Excuse me, is there a bank in the university?

B: Yes, there is.

A: Where is it?

B: It is right ahead.

A: Is it far from here?

B: No, it isn't. It's about five minutes' walk from here.

A: Can you tell me how to get there?

B: Go straight ahead. The bank is on the left side of the road.

A: Thank you!

B: You're welcome.

## （二）骑车去或者走路去，都行

（上午八点，松山准备去教室上课……）

Cháng Hào: Sōngshān, jīntiān nǐ qù jiàoshì shàng kè ma?
常浩：松山，今天你去教室上课吗？

Sōngshān: Qù ya.
松山：去呀。

Cháng Hào: Yǔ zhème dà, zěnme qù ya?
常浩：雨这么大，怎么去呀？

Sōngshān: Qí chē qù huòzhě zǒulù qù, dōu xíng!
松山：骑车去或者走路去，都行！

Cháng Hào: Nǐ qí diàndòngchē qù ba, wǒ de tuǐ háishi bù néng zǒu, nǐ dàishang wǒ, kěyǐ ma?
常浩：你骑电动车去吧，我的腿还是不能走，你带上我，可以吗？

Sōngshān: Dāngrán kěyǐ. Shàng chē ba. Nǐ yòng zhè bǎ yǔsǎn, wǒ chuān yǔyī.
松山：当然可以。（骑上电动车）上车吧。你用这把雨伞，我穿雨衣。

Cháng Hào: Hǎo, xièxie nǐ!
常浩：好，谢谢你！

Sōngshān: Bú kèqi.
松山：不客气。

---

**We can go there by bike or on foot**

(At eight o'clock in the morning, Matsuyama was ready to go to class...)

Chang Hao: Matsuyama, are you going to class today?

Matsuyama: Yes, I am.

Chang Hao: It's raining hard. How can you get to the classroom?
Matsuyama: We can go there by bike or on foot.
Chang Hao: I'll still can't walk. Could you ride an electric bike and take me?
Matsuyama: Sure. (Matsuyama gets on the electric bike) Come on up. You take this umbrella. I'll wear a raincoat.
Chang Hao: OK, thank you!
Matsuyama: You're welcome.

## 二 生词 New Words

| | | | | |
|---|---|---|---|---|
| 1 | 告诉 | gàosu | 动 | to tell |
| 2 | 里边 | lǐbian | 名 | inside; in |
| 3 | 银行 | yínháng | 名 | bank |
| 4 | 前边 | qiánbian | 名 | in front; ahead |
| 5 | 离 | lí | 动 | to be away from |
| 6 | 远 | yuǎn | 形 | far; distant |
| 7 | 大概 | dàgài | 副 | probably |
| 8 | 分钟 | fēnzhōng | 量 | minute |
| 9 | 一直 | yìzhí | 副 | all the time; straight |
| 10 | 往 | wǎng | 介 | to; towards |
| 11 | 前 | qián | 名 | front |
| 12 | 马路 | mǎlù | 名 | road |
| 13 | 左边 | zuǒbian | 名 | left side |
| | 右边 | yòubian | 名 | right side |
| 14 | 骑 | qí | 动 | to ride |
| 15 | 或者 | huòzhě | 连 | or |
| 16 | 教室 | jiàoshì | 名 | classroom |
| 17 | 雨 | yǔ | 名 | rain |

# 第十九课 Lesson 19

| 18 | 这么 | zhème | 代 | so; such; like this |
| 19 | 电动车 | diàndòngchē | 名 | electric bicycle |
| 20 | 腿 | tuǐ | 名 | leg |
| 21 | 还是 | háishi | 副 | still; yet |
| 22 | 带 | dài | 动 | to take; to bring |
| 23 | 上 | shàng | 动 | *used as a complement after a verb* |
| 24 | 上车 | shàng chē | | to get on the vehicle |
| 25 | 雨伞 | yǔsǎn | 名 | umbrella |
| 26 | 穿 | chuān | 动 | to wear |
| 27 | 雨衣 | yǔyī | 名 | raincoat |

## 专名 Zhuānmíng  Proper Nouns

| 1 | 松山 | Sōngshān | Matsuyama, a Japanese student |
| 2 | 常浩 | Cháng Hào | Chang Hao, a student |

## 三 注释 Notes

| 方位词 | 前边 | 后边 | 左边 | 右边 | 上边 | 下边 | 东边 | 西边 | 南边 | 北边 | 中间 | 旁边 |

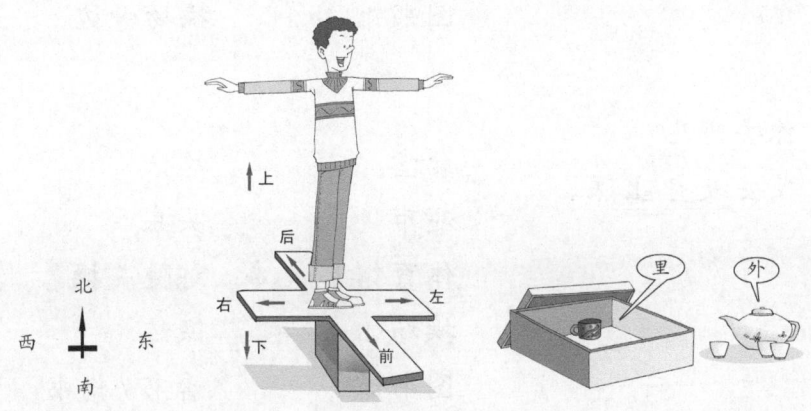

## 四 练习 Exercises

**（一）朗读下列发音相近的词语** Read aloud the following words and expressions with similar pronunciation

| yínháng | yǐnháng | dàgài | dà gǎi |
|---|---|---|---|
| 银行 | 引吭 | 大概 | 大改 |
| gàosu | gāosù | yìzhí | yìzhì |
| 告诉 | 高速 | 一直 | 意志 |
| huòzhě | huózhe | yǔyī | yǔyì |
| 或者 | 活着 | 雨衣 | 语义 |

**（二）替换并朗读** Replace and read aloud

1. 学校里边有<u>银行</u>吗？

   邮局　体育馆　医院　理发店
   商店　咖啡馆　饭馆/饭店　超市

2. A：请问，<u>留学生公寓</u>在哪儿？
   B：在<u>马路左边</u>。

   | 教学楼 | 操场东边 |
   |---|---|
   | 体育馆 | 食堂西边 |
   | 食堂 | 教学楼和体育馆中间 |
   | 超市 | 图书馆南边 |
   | 操场/运动场 | 办公楼北边 |
   | 图书馆 | 操场旁边 |

3. A：你去哪儿？
   B：我去<u>教室</u> <u>上课</u>。

   | 食堂 | 吃饭 |
   |---|---|
   | 超市 | 买东西 |
   | 体育馆 | 练健美操 |
   | 操场 | 锻炼 |
   | 图书馆 | 看书/借书 |

（三）选词填空并朗读下列句子 Choose the appropriate words to fill in the blanks and read aloud the following sentences

> 往　　有　　怎么　　离　　在

1. A：请问，学校里边_____银行吗？
   B：有啊。
2. A：银行_____哪儿？
   B：就在前边。
3. A：_____这儿远吗？
   B：离这儿不远。
4. 你能告诉我到那儿_____走吗？
5. 你从这儿一直_____前走，银行就在马路左边。

> 怎么　　上　　去　　或者　　还是

1. 上午八点，常浩准备_____教室上课。
2. 雨这么大，咱们_____去教室呀？
3. 骑车去_____走路去，都行！
4. 你骑电动车去吧，我的腿_____不能走，你带上我，可以吗？
5. 当然可以，_____车吧。

（四）边做边说 Act and say

A：你的前边/后边/左边/右边……是谁？
B：我的前边是玛丽/安丽/阿里/马丁……。

（五）和同学一起表演以下会话 Act out the conversation with your classmates

A：劳驾，请问附近有超市吗？
B：超市就在前边。
A：离这儿远吗？
B：不远，走路去，五分钟就到了。

A：能告诉我怎么走吗？

B：你从这儿一直往前走，到红绿灯那儿往左拐，见到一座白色大楼，那就是超市。

A：啊，知道了。谢谢您！

B：不客气。

（六）根据实际情况回答问题 Answer the questions according to the actual situations

1. 你们学校里边有银行（邮局/体育馆/医院/理发店/超市/咖啡馆）吗？
2. 你们学校的教学楼（图书馆/食堂/体育馆/运动场/留学生公寓/超市）在哪儿？

（七）和同学一起表演课文 Act out the text with your classmates

（八）读后说 Read the passage and say it

早上下雨，雨很大。

我问同学松山怎么去上课，他说骑车去或者走路去都行。我说："你骑电动车去吧，我的腿还是不能走，你带我去教室，可以吗？"他说："当然可以。"

他穿雨衣，我打伞，他骑车带我去教室上课。我很感谢他。

（九）怎么表达 How to express

| tóngyì |
| 同意 agreement |

Zánmen zǒulù qù, xíng bu xíng?
1. A：咱们 走路去，行 不 行？

Can we go there on foot?

Xíng!
B：行！

All right!

2. A： Nǐ gāngcái dú de nà shǒu shī hěn hǎo, néng bu néng gěi wǒ kànkan?
你 刚才 读的 那 首 诗 很 好，能 不 能 给 我 看看？

The poem you just read is very good. Can I have a look?

B： Kěyǐ.
可以。

OK.

（十）朗读中国经典诗词，请注意语音语调 Read aloud the classic Chinese poem and pay attention to the pronunciation and intonation

Zèng Wāng Lún
赠 汪 伦

[Táng] Lǐ Bái
[唐] 李 白（701—762）

Lǐ Bái chéng zhōu jiāng yù xíng, hū wén àn shang tàgē shēng.
李白 乘 舟 将 欲 行，忽 闻 岸 上 踏歌声。

Táohuā Tán shuǐ shēn qiān chǐ, bù jí Wāng Lún sòng wǒ qíng.
桃花 潭 水 深 千 尺，不 及 汪 伦 送 我 情。

（十一）请欣赏下列著名的词句 Please enjoy the following famous saying

Zhù rén wéi lè.
助人为乐。

Take pleasure in helping people.

# 第二十课 Lesson 20

## Dì-èrshí kè
## Wǒ xiǎng kāi yí gè huóqī zhànghù
## 我想开一个活期账户
## I'd like to open a current account

### 一 课文 Text

（一）我想开一个活期账户

（在银行）

Yíngyèyuán: Qǐngwèn, nín yào bàn shénme yèwù?
营业员：请问，您要办什么业务？

Mǎdīng: Wǒ xiǎng kāi yí gè huóqī zhànghù.
马丁：我想开一个活期账户。

Yíngyèyuán: Qǐng gěi wǒ nín de hùzhào.
营业员：请给我您的护照。

Mǎdīng: Gěi nín.
马丁：给您。

Yíngyèyuán: Qǐng tián yíxiàr zhè zhāng biǎo.
营业员：请填一下儿这张表。

Mǎdīng: Hǎo de. Zhèyàng kěyǐ ma?
马丁：好的。这样可以吗？

Yíngyèyuán: Kěyǐ. Qǐng nín shūrù yí gè mìmǎ.
营业员：可以。请您输入一个密码。

Mǎdīng: Hǎo de.
马丁：好的。

Yíngyèyuán: Qǐng zài shūrù yí cì. Hǎo, zhè shì nín de cúnzhé hé yínhángkǎ.
营业员：请再输入一次。好，这是您的存折和银行卡。

---

I'd like to open a current account

(At the bank)

Bank clerk: What can I do for you?

Martin: I'd like to open a current account.

Bank clerk: Give me your passport, please.

Martin: Here you are.

Bank clerk: Please fill in this form.

Martin: All right. Like this, right?

Bank clerk: Yes. Please enter a password.

Martin: OK.

Bank clerk: Please enter it again. OK, here are your passbook and bank card.

## （二）能帮我开通手机银行吗

营业员：您还办别的业务吗？

马丁：能帮我开通手机银行吗？

营业员：当然可以。请告诉我您的手机号。

马丁：135****0987。

营业员：请您看一下儿镜头。

马丁：要拍照吗？

营业员：对。请您输入一个密码。再输一次。好了，您看一下儿手机。

马丁：可以了。

---

**Can you help me open the mobile banking service**

Bank clerk: Is there anything else I can do for you?

Martin: Can you help me open the mobile banking service?

Bank clerk: Of course. Please tell me your mobile phone number.

Martin: 135****0987.

Bank clerk: Please look at the camera.

Martin: Do we need a photo?

Bank clerk: Yes. Please enter your password. Please enter it again. All right. Please check it on your phone.

Martin: I've got the service.

## 二 生词 New Words

| | | | | |
|---|---|---|---|---|
| 1 | 开 | kāi | 动 | to open (an account in a bank) |
| 2 | 活期 | huóqī | 形 | due on demand |
| 3 | 账户 | zhànghù | 名 | account |
| 4 | 营业员 | yíngyèyuán | 名 | (bank) clerk |
| 5 | 办 | bàn | 动 | to do; to handle |
| 6 | 业务 | yèwù | 名 | business |
| 7 | 护照 | hùzhào | 名 | passport |
| 8 | 填表 | tián biǎo | | to fill in a form |
| | 表 | biǎo | 名 | form |
| 9 | 张 | zhāng | 量 | (a measure word for paper, drawings, etc.) piece; sheet |
| 10 | 输入密码 | shūrù mìmǎ | | to enter a password |
| | 输入 | shūrù | 动 | to input |
| | 密码 | mìmǎ | 名 | password |
| 11 | 次 | cì | 量 | (a measure word for repeated occurrences or events likely to be repeated) time(s) |
| 12 | 存折 | cúnzhé | 名 | bankbook |
| 13 | 银行卡 | yínhángkǎ | 名 | bank card |
| 14 | 别的 | biéde | 代 | other |
| 15 | 开通 | kāitōng | 动 | to open (a service) |
| 16 | 手机 | shǒujī | 名 | mobile phone; cell phone |
| | 拍照 | pāi zhào | 动 | to take a photo |

# 第二十课 Lesson 20

## 三 练习 Exercises

**(一) 朗读 Read aloud**

1. 朗读下列发音相近的词语 Read aloud the following words and expressions with similar pronunciation

| huóqī | héqi | zhànghù | shāngpù |
|---|---|---|---|
| 活期 | 和气 | 账户 | 商铺 |

| hùzhào | hūjiào | biéde | xié de |
|---|---|---|---|
| 护照 | 呼叫 | 别的 | 斜的 |

| cúnzhé | zhǔnzé | shūrù | chūrù |
|---|---|---|---|
| 存折 | 准则 | 输入 | 出入 |

2. 朗读下列打油诗 Read the following doggerel aloud

Zhǐyào nǐ xǐhuan, Hànyǔ bìng bù nán.
只要你喜欢，汉语并不难。

Jiānchí qù shàng kè, zuòyè ànshí wán.
坚持去上课，作业按时完。

Shēngcí dōu jìzhù, kèwén dú shí biàn.
生词都记住，课文读十遍。

Dàyuē yì nián hòu, kěyǐ suíxīn tán.
大约一年后，可以随心谈。

Chinese is not difficult as long as you like it.

Go to class every day and finish homework on time.

Remember all the new words. Read the text ten times.

After about a year, you can talk as you like.

**(二) 替换并朗读 Replace and read aloud**

1. A：您要办什么业务？
   B：我想<u>开一个活期账户</u>。

   换钱　存钱　取钱　转账
   开通手机银行 / 网上银行

2. <u>能帮我开通手机银行吗</u>？

   换点儿钱　　取点儿钱
   转一下儿账　帮我一个忙
   教教我怎么用

（三）选词填空并朗读下列句子 Choose the appropriate words to fill in the blanks and read aloud the following sentences

> 护照　　再　　和　　办　　密码

1. 请问，您要_____什么业务？
2. 请给我您的_____。
3. 请输入您的_____。请您_____输入一次。
4. 这是您的存折_____银行卡。

> 输入　　告诉　　镜头　　还　　开通

1. 您_____办别的业务吗？
2. 能帮我_____手机银行吗？
3. 当然可以。请_____我您的手机号。
4. 请您看这个_____。
5. 请您_____一个密码，请您再输入一次。

（四）你是 A，请你向 B 提问 Supposing you are A, ask B questions

A: _____？（做什么）
B: 我去银行开活期账户。
A: _____？（什么）
B: 要带护照。
A: _____？（密码）
B: 要输入一个密码。
A: _____？（几）
B: 密码要输入两次。
A: _____？（还　办）
B: 我还要开通手机银行。
A: _____？（什么）
B: 需要手机号。

A：_____？（还）

B：还要给我拍照。

A：_____？（吗）

B：都要输入密码。

（五）和同学练习以下会话 Practice the following conversation with your classmates

A：你好，你要办什么业务？

B：我存钱也换钱。

A：你要存什么钱？

B：我存美元。

A：你存多少？

B：我要存一千美元，换五百美元的人民币。

（六）和同学一起表演课文 Act out the text with your classmates

（七）读后说 Read the passage and say it

今天我去银行，营业员问我要办什么业务，我说我要开一个活期账户。营业员要我给他护照，还要我填一张表。他给了我一个存折和一张银行卡。他问我还办别的业务吗，我说我想开通手机银行，他说当然可以。他要我告诉他手机号，还要拍照，还要输入两次密码。

（八）怎么表达 How to express

qǐngqiú (2)
请求（2） request (2)

Bāng wǒ yí gè máng, hǎo ma?
1. 帮 我一个 忙，好吗？

Would you please do me a favor?

Qǐng bāng wǒ dǎyìn yíxiàr zhège wénjiàn, hǎoma?
2. 请 帮 我打印 一下儿 这个 文件，好吗？

Could you print this document for me, please?

（九）朗读中国经典诗词，请注意语音语调 Read aloud the classic Chinese poem and pay attention to the pronunciation and intonation

### Jiāng Xuě
### 江 雪

[Táng] Liǔ Zōngyuán
[唐] 柳 宗元（773—819）

Qiān shān niǎo fēi jué, wàn jìng rén zōng miè.
千 山 鸟 飞 绝，万 径 人 踪 灭。

Gū zhōu suō lì wēng, dú diào hán jiāng xuě.
孤 舟 蓑 笠 翁，独 钓 寒 江 雪。

（十）请欣赏下列著名的词句 Please enjoy the following famous saying

Jìngrénzhě, rén héng jìng zhī.
敬人者，人 恒 敬 之。

Respect others and they will respect you.

# 第二十一课 Lesson 21
## Dì-èrshíyī kè 我每天都过得很愉快
### Wǒ měi tiān dōu guòde hěn yúkuài
### I'm having a good time every day

## 一 课文 Text

（玛丽跟爸爸妈妈视频聊天儿……）

Bàba: Zěnmeyàng a, Mǎlì?
爸爸：怎么样啊，玛丽？

Mǎlì: Bàba māma, nǐmen fàng xīn ba, wǒ měi tiān dōu guòde hěn yúkuài.
玛丽：爸爸妈妈，你们放心吧，我每天都过得很愉快。

Māma: Nǐmen bān yǒu duōshao rén?
妈妈：你们班有多少人？

Mǎlì: Shíbā ge.
玛丽：十八个。

Māma: Dōu shì nǎxiē guójiā de?
妈妈：都是哪些国家的？

Mǎlì: Kě duō le. Shíbā ge tóngxué láizì shísān ge guójiā.
玛丽：可多了。十八个同学来自十三个国家。

Māma: À, nàme duō guójiā ya. Nǐmen xiāngchǔ de zěnmeyàng a?
妈妈：啊，那么多国家呀。你们相处得怎么样啊？

Mǎlì: Tèbié hǎo! Wǒmen bān shì yí ge héxié de dà jiātíng, tóngxuémen hùxiāng
玛丽：特别好！我们班是一个和谐的大家庭，同学们互相
guānxīn、hùxiāng bāngzhù, xiàng xiōngdì jiěmèi yíyàng. Wǒ ài zhège bān,
关心、互相帮助，像兄弟姐妹一样。我爱这个班，
wǒ xǐhuan wǒ de tóngxuémen.
我喜欢我的同学们。

Bàba: Nà tài hǎo le, nǐ zhēn shì xìngyùn!
爸爸：那太好了，你真是幸运！

Mǎlì: Bàba, gèng xìngyùn de shì, jiāo wǒmen de liǎng wèi lǎoshī yě hěn hǎo.
玛丽：爸爸，更幸运的是，教我们的两位老师也很好。

Tāmen jiāo kè fēicháng rènzhēn yě fēicháng yǒu nàixīn, duì wǒmen fēicháng
他们教课非常认真也非常有耐心，对我们非常

qīnqiè yě fēicháng rèqíng. Tāmen jì shì lǎoshī, yě shì wǒmen de péngyou,
亲切也非常热情。他们既是老师，也是我们的朋友，

wúwēi-búzhì de guān'ài zhe wǒmen.
无微不至地关爱着我们。

Bàba: Tīng nǐ zhème shuō, wǒ yě xiǎng dào nǐmen bān qù shàng kè.
爸爸：听你这么说，我也想到你们班去上课。

Mǎlì: Wǒ zhēn xīwàng bàba māma kuài dào Zhōngguó lái kànkan.
玛丽：我真希望爸爸妈妈快到中国来看看。

---

**I have a good time every day**

(Mary is video chatting with her parents...)

Dad: How are you, Mary?

Mary: Mom, Dad, don't worry. I have a good time every day.

Mom: How many students are there in your class?

Mary: Eighteen.

Mom: What countries are they from?

Mary: Many countries. The eighteen students come from thirteen countries.

Mom: Ah, so many countries. How are you getting along?

Mary: Very well. Our class is a harmonious big family. We care about each other and help each other, like brothers and sisters. I love this class. I like my classmates.

Dad: That's great. You are so lucky.

Mary: What's more, the two teachers who teach us are also very good. They teach very carefully and patiently. They are very kind and warm-hearted to us. They are our teachers as well as our friends. They take good care of us.

Dad: What you said makes me also want to go to your class.

Mary: I wish Mom and Dad could come to China to have a look soon.

## 二 生词 New Words

| | | | | |
|---|---|---|---|---|
| 1 | 过 | guò | 动 | to spend (time); to pass (time) |
| 2 | 愉快 | yúkuài | 形 | happy; cheerful |

## 第二十一课 Lesson 21

| | | | | |
|---|---|---|---|---|
| 3 | 放心 | fàng xīn | 动 | to be at ease; to feel relieved |
| 4 | 班 | bān | 名 | class |
| 5 | 国家 | guójiā | 名 | country |
| 6 | 来自 | láizì | 动 | to come from |
| 7 | 特别 | tèbié | 副、形 | especially; special |
| 8 | 和谐 | héxié | 形 | harmonious |
| 9 | 家庭 | jiātíng | 名 | family |
| 10 | 关心 | guānxīn | 动 | to care about |
| 11 | 帮助 | bāngzhù | 动 | to help |
| 12 | 兄弟 | xiōngdì | 名 | brother |
| 13 | 姐妹 | jiěmèi | 名 | sister |
| 14 | 更 | gèng | 副 | even more |
| 15 | 教 | jiāo | 动 | to teach |
| 16 | 认真 | rènzhēn | 形 | earnest; careful |
| 17 | 耐心 | nàixīn | 名、形 | patience; patient (with sth. or sb.) |
| 18 | 亲切 | qīnqiè | 形 | kind; cordial |
| 19 | 热情 | rèqíng | 形 | enthusiastic; zealous; warm |
| 20 | 既 | jì | 副 | used correlatively with adverb 也 yě, 又 yòu, etc., to show two situations are available |
| 21 | 无微不至 | wúwēi-búzhì | | meticulously |
| 22 | 地 | de | 助 | used after an adjective or phrase to form an adverbial adjunct before a verb |
| 23 | 关爱 | guān'ài | 动 | to care and love |
| 24 | 希望 | xīwàng | 动、名 | hope |

## 三 注释 Notes

（一）我每天都过得很愉快。

"动词+得+很+形容词"的功能是描述或评价动作行为的结果、程度和状态。例如：

The function of "V + 得 + 很 + Adj" is to describe or evaluate the result, degree and state of an action. For example:

1. 你读得很好。
2. 我们相处得很好。
3. 他学得很努力。

（二）助词"地"表示它前面的词或词组是状语。The particle " 地 " means that the word or phrase before it is an adverbial.

1. 他们是老师，也是我们的朋友，无微不至地关爱着我们。
2. 她每天都高高兴兴地去上课。

## 四 练习 Exercises

（一）朗读 Read aloud

1. 朗读下列发音相近的词语 Read aloud the following words and expressions with similar pronunciation

| guānxīn | gānxīn | xiōngdì | xīndì |
| 关心 | 甘心 | 兄弟 | 心地 |
| héxié | héjiě | zhēn shì | zhēnshí |
| 和谐 | 和解 | 真 是 | 真实 |
| kànkan | hǎnhan | xīwàng | qīwàng |
| 看看 | 喊喊 | 希望 | 期望 |

2. 朗读下列词组 Read the following phrases aloud

跟爸爸视频　　跟朋友视频　　跟同学视频

你怎么样　　你们班怎么样　　爸爸怎么样

## 第二十一课 Lesson 21

| 妈妈怎么样 | 爷爷怎么样 | 奶奶怎么样 | |
| 像兄弟一样 | 像姐妹一样 | 像爸爸妈妈一样 | |
| 互相关心 | 互相帮助 | 互相学习 | 互相关爱 |
| 太好了 | 太高兴了 | 太幸运了 | 太对了 |
| 太快了 | 太慢了 | 太忙了 | 太难了 |

（二）替换并朗读 Replace and read aloud

1. 我每天都<u>过得很愉快</u>。

> 生活得很愉快　学得很愉快
> 吃得很好　　　睡得很好
> 玩儿得很好

2. 你们<u>相处</u>得怎么样啊？

> 学　　说　　读
> 吃　　生活　练习

3. <u>他们既是我们的老师，也/又是我们的朋友</u>。

> 他　　　聪明　　　　　　努力
> 班长　　是老师的帮手　　是同学们的好朋友
> 同学们　要努力学习　　　要好好锻炼身体
> 我　　　喜欢吃米饭　　　喜欢吃面条儿
> 他　　　会学习　　　　　很会玩儿
> 我们　　要了解中国的今天　要了解中国的昨天

（三）选词填空并朗读下列句子 Choose the appropriate words to fill in the blanks and read aloud the following sentences

> 希望　对　都　也　这么　幸运　来自　一样

1. 爸爸妈妈，你们放心吧，我每天_____过得很愉快。
2. A：你们班有多少人？
   B：我们班有十八个同学，_____十三个国家。

3. 我们相处得特别好！同学们互相关心、互相帮助，像兄弟姐妹_____。我爱这个班，我喜欢我的同学们。

4. 那太好了，你真是_____！

5. 更幸运的是，教我们的两位老师都很好。他们教课非常认真也非常有耐心，_____我们非常亲切也非常热情。

6. 他们既是老师，_____是我们的朋友，无微不至地关爱着我们。

7. 听你_____说，我也想到你们班去上课。

8. 我真_____爸爸妈妈快到中国来看看。

（四）选择合适的词组填空，完成一个句子 Choose the appropriate phrases to complete the sentences.

做练习　说话　喝啤酒　看书　拥抱　聊天儿

1. 同学们在愉快地_____。
2. 她们一见面就热情地_____。
3. 同学们在图书馆安静地_____。
4. 她俩在小声地_____。
5. 我们一起高兴地_____。
6. 她在努力地_____。

苹果一样　　真的一样　　　冬天一样冷
花园一样　　运动员一样快　姐姐一样好

1. 我们的学校像_____。
2. 今天天气像_____。
3. 她的脸红得像_____。
4. 他画的马像_____。
5. 她对我像_____。
6. 他跑得像_____。

（提示：生词请查阅各类词典。）

(Tip: For new words, please refer to various dictionaries.)

（五）把 A 列与 B 列连线，组成一个句子，然后朗读 Match A with B to make sentences and then read the sentences aloud

| A | B |
|---|---|
| 我学得 | 很早。 |
| 我每天都过得 | 很慢，也很清楚。 |
| 他练习做得 | 很努力，也很快乐。 |
| 我们俩好得 | 很愉快。 |
| 课堂上老师说得 | 很好。 |
| 他每天早上都起得 | 像姐妹一样。 |

（六）根据实际情况回答问题 Answer the questions according to the actual situations

1. 你常常跟爸爸妈妈视频聊天儿吗？
2. 你们班有多少男同学？多少女同学？
3. 你们班的同学都来自哪些国家？
4. 你们有几位老师？
5. 你觉得你们班怎么样？

（七）和同学一起表演课文 Act out the text with your classmates

（八）读后说 Read the passage and say it

今天我跟爸爸妈妈视频聊天儿。爸爸妈妈问这问那，我们聊得非常高兴。我对他们说，你们放心吧，我在这儿每天都过得很愉快。

我给他们介绍了我们班的情况。

我们班一共十八个人，来自十三个国家。全班同学互相关心、互相帮助，像兄弟姐妹一样。我爱我的班，我喜欢我的同学们。

爸爸说我真幸运。我说，更幸运的是，教我们的两位老师都很好，他们教课非常认真也非常有耐心，对我们非常亲切也非常热情。他们既是老师，又是我们的朋友，无微不至地关爱着我们。

爸爸很高兴,听我这么说,也想到我们班来上课。我说,希望爸爸妈妈快到中国来看看。

(九) 怎么表达 How to express

> bàoxiū
> 报修　request for repair

A：Shì wùyè zhōngxīn ma?
　　是 物业 中心 吗?
　　Is this the property management center?

B：Shì.
　　是。
　　Yes.

A：Wǒ fángjiān wèishēngjiān de shuǐguǎn lòu shuǐ, qǐng jiào rén lái xiūlǐ yíxiàr.
　　我 房间 卫生间 的 水管 漏水,请 叫人来修理一下儿。
　　The water pipe in my bathroom is leaking. Please call someone to fix it.

(十) 朗读中国经典诗词,请注意语音语调 Read aloud the classic Chinese poem and pay attention to the pronunciation and intonation

Yóuzǐ Yín
游子吟

[Táng] Mèng Jiāo
[唐] 孟 郊 (751—814)

Cí mǔ shǒu zhōng xiàn, yóuzǐ shēn shang yī.
慈母手中线,游子身上衣。

Lín xíng mìmì féng, yì kǒng chíchí guī.
临行密密缝,意恐迟迟归。

Shuí yán cùn cǎo xīn, bào dé sān chūn huī.
谁言寸草心,报得三春晖。

# 第二十一课 Lesson 21

（十一）请欣赏下列著名的词句 Please enjoy the following famous saying

Yǒu péng zì yuǎnfāng lái, búyìlèhū?<br>
有 朋 自 远方 来，不亦乐乎？<br>
Isn't not a joy to have friends coming from afar?

# 第二十二课 Lesson 22
## 想成才就必须多读书
### Xiǎng chéngcái jiù bìxū duō dú shū
### You have to read more books to be successful

## 一 课文 Text

（两个留学生在聊天儿……）

A：Nǐ cháng qù xuéxiào túshūguǎn ma?
你常去学校图书馆吗？

B：Cháng qù.
常去。

A：Jièguo shū ma?
借过书吗？

B：Méiyǒu. Wǒ zhǐ zài yuèlǎnshì kàn shū, hái méiyǒu jièguo shū. Nǐ ne?
没有。我只在阅览室看书，还没有借过书。你呢？

A：Hěn cánkuì, lái zhèr yǐhòu, wǒ hái méi qùguo túshūguǎn ne. Zuótiān shàng kè, lǎoshī shuō, yào xiǎng chéngcái, bìxū yào dú dàliàng de shū. Lǎoshī hái yào wǒmen yǒu zìxué de nénglì, wǒ cái xiǎng qù túshūguǎn kànkan.
很惭愧，来这儿以后，我还没去过图书馆呢。昨天上课，老师说，要想成才，必须要读大量的书。老师还要我们有自学的能力，我才想去图书馆看看。

B：Zánmen xuéxiào de túshūguǎn hěn hǎo. Búguò, wǒ juéde zìjǐ de Hànyǔ shuǐpíng hěn dī, hái bù néng dú Zhōngwén shū, suǒyǐ wǒ méiyǒu jièguo shū.
咱们学校的图书馆很好。不过，我觉得自己的汉语水平很低，还不能读中文书，所以我没有借过书。

A：Yí ge xuésheng yàoshi xuéxiào túshūguǎn dōu méiyǒu qùguo, jiù tài bù hǎoyì-
一个学生要是学校图书馆都没有去过，就太不好意

## Lesson 22 第二十二课

<pre>
         si le.    Wǒ xiǎng,  bùguǎn gōngkè duō máng,  yě yīnggāi chōu shíjiān dú diǎnr
    思了。我 想， 不管 功课 多 忙，也 应该 抽 时间 读点儿
         kèwài shū.
    课外 书。

         Nǐ shuōde duì.   Nǐ yào zài  zhèr  xué duō cháng shíjiān?
 B：你 说得 对。你 要 在 这儿 学 多 长 时间？

         Gōngsī zhǐ ràng wǒ dú yì nián.
 A：公司 只 让 我读一年。

         Yì nián hěn kuài jiù guòqu le.
 B：一年 很 快 就过去了。

         Shì.    Suǒyǐ wǒ yào zhuājǐn shíjiān,   zhēngqǔ Hànyǔ tīng shuō nénglì yǒu jiào dà
 A：是。所以 我要 抓紧 时间， 争取 汉语 听 说 能力有 较 大
         de jìnbù.
    的进步。

         Nǐ hěn nǔlì,    xuéde yě hěn hǎo.
 B：你 很努力，学得 也 很 好。

         Nǎlǐ.    Nǐ guòjiǎng le.
 A：哪里。你 过奖了。
</pre>

---

**You have to read more books to be successful**

(Two international students are chatting...)

A: Do you often go to the school library?

B: Yes, I do.

A: Have you ever borrowed any books?

B: No, I haven't . I only read books in the reading room. I haven't borrowed any books yet. How about you?

A: I'm ashamed that I haven't been to the library since I came here. The teacher said in class yesterday that one must read a lot if he wants to be successful. The teacher wants us to have the ability of self-study. That's why I want to check out the library.

B: The library of our university is very good, but I think my Chinese level is too low for me to read Chinese books, so I haven't borrowed any books.

A: It would be a shame for a student to have never been to the school library. I think no matter how busy I am with my lessons, I should spare some time to read some books outside class.

B: You're right. How long will you study here?

A: The company only gave me one year to study.

B: A year goes by quickly.

A: Yes, so I must seize the time, striving for greater improvement in my Chinese listening and speaking skills.

B: You're working very hard and doing very well.
A: You flatter me.

## 二  生词 New Words

| 1 | 图书馆 | túshūguǎn | 名 | library |
|---|---|---|---|---|
|  | 书 | shū | 名 | book |
| 2 | 借 | jiè | 动 | to borrow |
| 3 | 阅览室 | yuèlǎnshì | 名 | reading room |
| 4 | 惭愧 | cánkuì | 形 | ashamed |
| 5 | 成才 | chéngcái | 动 | to become a useful person |
| 6 | 必须 | bìxū | 副 | must |
| 7 | 大量 | dàliàng | 形 | a large number of |
| 8 | 自学 | zìxué | 动 | to study on one's own |
| 9 | 能力 | nénglì | 名 | capacity; ability |
| 10 | 不过 | búguò | 连 | but; however |
| 11 | 水平 | shuǐpíng | 名 | level; standard |
| 12 | 低 | dī | 形 | low |
| 13 | 要是 | yàoshi | 连 | if; in case |
| 14 | 不好意思 | bù hǎoyìsi |  | embarrassed; awkward |
| 15 | 不管 | bùguǎn | 连 | no matter (what, how, etc.) |
| 16 | 功课 | gōngkè | 名 | homework; lesson; schoolwork |
| 17 | 课外 | kèwài | 名 | after school; outside class |
| 18 | 多 | duō | 代 | how; what |
| 19 | 长 | cháng | 形 | long |
| 20 | 时间 | shíjiān | 名 | time |

| 21 | 公司 | gōngsī | 名 | company; firm |
| 22 | 让 | ràng | 动 | to let; to allow |
| 23 | 快 | kuài | 形 | fast |
| 24 | 抓紧 | zhuājǐn | 动 | to firmly grasp; to lose no time |
| 25 | 争取 | zhēngqǔ | 动 | to strive for; to endeavor to |
| 26 | 较 | jiào | 副 | relatively; rather; quite |
| 27 | 进步 | jìnbù | 动 | to progress; to advance; to step forward |
| 28 | 过奖 | guòjiǎng | 动 | to flatter (sb.) |

## 三 注释 Notes

(一) 疑问代词"多" The interrogative pronoun "多"

疑问代词"多"用在疑问句里，询问程度和数量。"多"后面多为积极性的形容词，如"大、长、高、远、粗、宽、重、厚"等。例如：

The interrogative pronoun "多" is used in interrogative sentences to inquire about degree and quantity. "多" is usually followed by positive adjectives, such as "大", "长", "高", "远", "粗", "宽", "重", "厚", etc. For example:

1. A：你要在这儿学多长时间？
   B：公司只让我读一年。
2. A：你有多高？
   B：我一米七五。

(二) 不管 no matter (what, how, etc.); regardless of

"不管"和"都"或"也"一起用，表示在任何条件下结果或结论都不会改变。

"不管" is used together with "都" or "也" in a sentence to emphasize that the result or conclusion will not change under any circumstances.

"不管"后边一般要求有表示任指的疑问代词"什么、哪儿、谁、多少、怎么"等或者具有选择关系的并列成分。例如：

"不管" is usually followed by an interrogative pronoun indicating general reference, such as "什么"、"哪儿"、"谁"、"多少"、"怎么", etc., or by parallel elements as alternatives. For example:

1. 不管你什么时候来，我都欢迎。
2. 不管有多大困难，我也不怕。

**注意：**

不能说：* 不管下雨我都去教室上课。

可以说：不管下多大的雨我都去教室上课。

（三）要是……就…… if..., (then)...

"要是……就……"连接两个分句，表示在假设情况下产生某种结果。例如：

"要是……就……" joins two clauses, indicating a certain result of a hypothetical condition. For example:

1. 要是公司同意，我就再学一年。
2. 要是想家，就跟爸爸妈妈视频聊天儿。
3. 你要是去，我就去。

## 四 练习 Exercises

（一）朗读 Read aloud

1. 读下列发音相近的词语 Read aloud the following words and expressions with similar pronunciation

| jiè shū | jiéshù | bùguǎn | bù guān |
| 借书 | 结束 | 不管 | 不关 |
| cánkuì | chànhuǐ | zhēngqǔ | zhěngqí |
| 惭愧 | 忏悔 | 争取 | 整齐 |
| chéngcái | chéngzài | gōngkè | gōngkē |
| 成才 | 承载 | 功课 | 工科 |

## 第二十二课 Lesson 22

2. 朗读下列词组 Read the following phrases aloud

借书　　　　借钱　　　　借车　　　　借东西
你说得对　　你说得好　　你说得是
抓紧时间　　抓紧工作　　抓紧学习　　抓紧复习
听说能力　　读写能力　　翻译能力　　口语能力
一年很快就过去了　一学期很快就过去了　一星期很快就过去了

（二）替换并朗读 Replace and read aloud

A：你要在这儿学多长时间？
B：我在这儿只学<u>一年</u>。

| 三个月 | 半年 |
| 两年 | 四年 |

A：你今年多大？
B：我<u>二十</u>岁。

| 十八 | 十九 | 二十一 |
| 二十二 | 二十三 | |

A：你有多高？
B：我<u>一米七五</u>。

| 一米五九 | 一米六 |
| 一米六三 | 一米七二 |
| 一米七八 | 一米八 |

A：那儿离这儿有多远？
B：<u>十多公里</u>。

很远
一百多公里
一千多公里
有两万多公里
不太远，可以骑车去

A：这个箱子有多重？
B：<u>十公斤</u>。

十一斤　　不到二十公斤
三十公斤

（三）选词填空并朗读下列句子 Choose the appropriate words to fill in the blanks and read aloud the following sentences

> 惭愧　多(么)　能　大量　在　都

1. 我只_____阅览室看书，还没有借过书。你呢？
2. 很_____，来这儿以后，我还没去过学校图书馆呢。
3. 昨天上课时老师说，要想成才，必须读_____的书。
4. 我觉得自己的汉语水平很低，还不_____读中文书，所以没有借过书。
5. 一个学生要是学校图书馆_____没有去过，就太不好意思了。
6. 我想，不管功课_____忙，也应该抽时间读点儿课外书。

（四）把A列与B列连线组成一个句子，然后朗读 Match A with B to make sentences and then read the sentences aloud

1. 不管

| A | B |
|---|---|
| 不管你什么时候来， | 他都按时到校上课。 |
| 一到节假日，不管哪个景区 | 我都欢迎。 |
| 不管到哪里， | 都有很多人。 |
| 不管贵不贵， | 因为我早就想去长城看看。 |
| 不管你去不去，我都要去， | 他都喜欢跟中国人说汉语。 |
| 不管天气好坏， | 我都要买这本词典。 |

2. 要是……就……

| A | B |
|---|---|
| 你要是喜欢它， | 我们还去不去公园？ |
| 要是你想去， | 你就帮我给花浇（jiāo, to water）点儿水。 |
| 明天要是下雨， | 就应该坚持（jiānchí, to insist）每天去上课。 |
| 要是我不在的时候， | 我就送给你。 |
| 你要是慢点儿说， | 就跟我们一起去吧。 |
| 要是想学好汉语， | 我就能听懂。 |

## 第二十二课 Lesson 22

（五）根据实际情况回答问题 Answer the questions according to the actual situations

1. 你去过学校图书馆吗？
2. 你现在有时间读课外书吗？
3. 你喜欢读什么课外书？
4. 你一年能读几本书？
5. 你现在能读什么中文书？
6. 你会查汉语字典/词典吗？

（六）和同学一起表演课文 Act out the text with your classmates

（七）读后说 Read the passage and say it

　　朋友问我去没去过学校图书馆，这让我觉得很不好意思。来这个大学以后，我只知道图书馆在什么地方，但是没有去过，当然也没有借过书。

　　昨天上课的时候，老师说，要想成才，就必须读很多书。老师还要我们有自学的能力。我这才想，应该去图书馆看看。

　　朋友说，他觉得自己的汉语水平很低，现在还不能看中文书。我也是这样想的。我觉得自己认识的汉字还太少，读中文书很难。但是又想，一个学生要是学校的图书馆都没有去过，也太说不过去了。所以，我要去图书馆看看。以后，不管是英文的还是中文的课外书，我都要抽时间多读一些。

（八）怎么表达 How to express

jiè dōngxi
借东西　borrowing stuff

　　　　　Wǒ kěyǐ yòng yíxiàr nǐ de bǐ ma?
1. 我可以用一下儿你的笔吗？
　　May I use your pen?

　　　　　Nǐ néng bu néng jiè gěi wǒ yì bǎ yǔsǎn?
2. 你能不能借给我一把雨伞？
　　Could you lend me an umbrella?

（九）朗读中国经典诗词，请注意语音语调 Read the classic Chinese poem and pay attention to the pronunciation and intonation

Chūn Xiǎo
## 春 晓

[Táng] Mèng Hàorán
[唐] 孟 浩然（689—740）

Chūn mián bùjué xiǎo, chùchù wén tí niǎo.
春 眠 不 觉 晓，处处 闻 啼 鸟。

Yè lái fēngyǔ shēng, huā luò zhī duōshǎo.
夜来 风雨 声，花 落 知 多少。

（十）请欣赏下列著名的词句 Please enjoy the following famous saying

Shū dào yòng shí fāng hèn shǎo.
书 到 用 时 方 恨 少。

Only when we need to use books, do we regret that we've read too little.

# 第二十三课 难怪你学得这么好
## Dì-èrshísān kè　Nánguài nǐ xuéde zhème hǎo
### Lesson 23　No wonder you learn so well

## 一　课文 Text

（一）难怪你学得这么好

A：你每天几点（钟）起床？
　　Nǐ měi tiān jǐ diǎn (zhōng) qǐ chuáng?

B：我每天六点半起床。
　　Wǒ měi tiān liù diǎn bàn qǐ chuáng.

A：啊，你怎么起得那么早？你起床以后做什么？
　　Á, nǐ zěnme qǐde nàme zǎo? Nǐ qǐ chuáng yǐhòu zuò shénme?

B：去卫生间刷牙、洗脸，有时候洗澡。
　　Qù wèishēngjiān shuā yá, xǐ liǎn, yǒushíhou xǐ zǎo.

A：然后呢？
　　Ránhòu ne?

B：吃早饭，然后去上课。
　　Chī zǎofàn, ránhòu qù shàng kè.

A：你每天都去上课吗？
　　Nǐ měi tiān dōu qù shàng kè ma?

B：当然啊！你每天不也是这样吗？
　　Dāngrán a! Nǐ měi tiān bù yě shì zhèyàng ma?

A：有时候早上我想睡懒觉，就不去上课。
　　Yǒushíhou zǎoshang wǒ xiǎng shuì lǎnjiào, jiù bú qù shàng kè.

B：还是应该天天去上课，老师说，学得好的学生都坚持天天上课。
　　Háishi yīnggāi tiāntiān qù shàng kè, lǎoshī shuō, xuéde hǎo de xuéshēng dōu jiānchí tiāntiān shàng kè.

　　　　　　　Nánguài nǐ Hànyǔ xuéde zhème hǎo!
A：难怪 你汉语学得 这么 好！

　　　　Nǎlǐ.
B：哪里。

---

No wonder you learn so well

A: What time do you get up every day?

B: I get up at 6:30 every day.

A: Wow, why do you get up so early? What do you do after you get up?

B: I go to the bathroom to brush my teeth, wash my face, and sometimes take a bath.

A: And then?

B: Then I have breakfast and go to class.

A: Do you go to class every day?

B: Of course! Isn't that what you do every day?

A: Sometimes I feel like sleeping in the morning, so I don't go to class.

B: We'd better go to class every day. The teacher says that all the students who learn well go to class every day.

A: No wonder you learn Chinese so well.

B: You flatter me.

## （二）你现在要去哪儿

　　　　Nǐ xiànzài yào qù  nǎr?
A：你现在 要 去哪儿？

　　　　Wǒ qù jiàoshì shàng kè,  nǐ bú qù ma?
B：我 去教室 上 课，你不去吗？

　　　　Wǒ yǒudiǎnr bù shūfu,  nǐ tì wǒ qǐng gè jià ba.
A：我有点儿不舒服，你替我 请 个假吧。

　　　　Nǐ yòu xiǎng táo kè a?  Háishi qù shàng kè ba,  hé dàjiā  yìqǐ shàng kè
B：你又 想 逃课啊？还是去 上 课吧，和大家一起上 课

duō kuàilè ya!
多 快乐呀！

　　　　Hǎo ba.
A：好 吧。

　　　　Zánmen yìqǐ zǒu ba.
B：咱们 一起走吧。

　　　　Zǒu.
A：走。

## 第二十三课 Lesson 23

---

**Where are you going**

A: Where are you going?

B: I'm going to class. You're not going?

A: I feel a little under the weather. Please ask for leave for me.

B: You want to skip class again? Let's go to class. How happy we are to have class with everyone!

A: Fine.

B: Let's go together.

A: Let's go.

## 二 生词 New Words

| | | | | |
|---|---|---|---|---|
| 1 | 难怪 | nánguài | 动、副 | no wonder; understandable |
| 2 | 点（钟） | diǎn(zhōng) | 量 | o'clock |
| 3 | 起床 | qǐ chuáng | 动 | to get up |
| 4 | 半 | bàn | 数 | half |
| 5 | 卫生间 | wèishēngjiān | 名 | bathroom; restroom; toilet |
| 6 | 刷 | shuā | 动 | to brush |
| 7 | 牙 | yá | 名 | tooth (*pl. teeth*) |
| 8 | 洗 | xǐ | 动 | to wash |
| 9 | 脸 | liǎn | 名 | face |
| 10 | 有时候 | yǒushíhou | 副 | sometimes |
| 11 | 洗澡 | xǐ zǎo | 动 | to take a bath |
| 12 | 早饭 | zǎofàn | 名 | breakfast |
| 13 | 早上 | zǎoshang | 名 | morning |
| 14 | 睡懒觉 | shuì lǎnjiào | | to get up late; to sleep in |
| | 睡觉 | shuì jiào | 动 | to sleep; to go to bed |
| | 懒 | lǎn | 形 | lazy |
| 15 | 还是 | háishi | 副 | (*expressing hope*) had better |

| 16 | 应该 | yīnggāi | 助动 | should; ought to |
| 17 | 坚持 | jiānchí | 动 | to insist |
| 18 | 舒服 | shūfu | 形 | well; comfortable |
| 19 | 替 | tì | 动 | for; in place of |
| 20 | 请假 | qǐng jià | 动 | to ask for leave |
| 21 | 逃课 | táo kè | 动 | to skip class |
| 22 | 多 | duō | 副 | how; to what extent |

## 三 注释 Notes

（一）你每天不也是这样吗？

这是一个反问句，意思是：你每天也是这样。

This is a rhetorical question, meaning you are the same as me every day.

（二）还是应该坚持天天上课。

句子中的"还是"表示比较后做出的选择，用于建议。例如：
"还是" in the sentence indicates the choice after comparison and is used for suggestions. For example:

1. 还是坐地铁（dìtiě, subway）好，不堵车（dǔ chē, traffic jam）。
2. 还是你说吧，我不会说。

（三）坚持天天上课。

某些单音节名词或量词重叠，有"每"的意思。例如：
Some monosyllabic nouns or measure words overlap, meaning "every." For example:

天天 = 每天　人人 = 每人　个个 = 每个

## 第二十三课 Lesson 23

### 四 练习 Exercises

（一）朗读下列发音相近的词语 Read aloud the following words and expressions with similar pronunciation

| měi tiān | méitián | jǐ diǎn | qǐdiǎn |
| 每 天 | 煤田 | 几点 | 起点 |

| qǐ chuáng | qìchuán | xǐ liǎn | xǐyàn |
| 起 床 | 汽船 | 洗脸 | 喜宴 |

| wèishēng | wěishēng | dāngrán | tǎnrán |
| 卫生 | 尾声 | 当然 | 坦然 |

（二）替换并朗读 Replace and read aloud

1. A：你每天几点起床？
   B：我每天六点半起床。

   | 吃早饭 | 七点 |
   | 去教室上课 | 八点／八点半 |
   | 吃午饭 | 十二点 |
   | 锻炼身体 | 下午四点以后 |
   | 吃晚饭 | 晚上七点 |
   | 做作业 | 八点 |
   | 睡觉 | 十点／十点多 |

2. A：然后你做什么？
   B：吃早饭，然后去上课。

   | 去操场锻炼 | 去教室上课 |
   | 去食堂吃午饭 | 听录音／做练习 |
   | 玩儿手机／上网／看视频 | 跟朋友聊天儿 |

3. A：你去哪儿？
   B：我去学校上课。

   | 去公园 | 玩儿 |
   | 去食堂 | 吃饭 |
   | 去体育馆／操场 | 锻炼 |
   | 去图书馆 | 看书／借书 |
   | 回宿舍 | 休息 |
   | 去超市 | 买东西 |

（三）选词填空并朗读下列句子 Choose the appropriate words to fill in the blanks and read aloud the following sentences

　　都　什么　这样　就　几　那么

1. A：你每天_____点（钟）起床？
　　B：我每天六点半起床。
2. 啊，你怎么起得_____早？
3. A：你起床以后做_____？
　　B：去卫生间刷牙、洗脸，有时候洗澡。
4. 你每天都去上课吗？当然啦！你每天不也是_____吗？
5. 有时候早上我想睡懒觉，_____不去上课。
6. 还是应该天天上课，老师说，学得好的学生_____坚持天天上课。

（四）将A、B两列连线，组成正确的对话，然后朗读 Match A with B to make up appropriate dialogues

1.　　　A　　　　　　　　　　　　　　　　　B

他汉语说得好吗？　　　　　　　　　　我每天都起得很早。
他游泳（yóu yǒng, to swim）游得怎么样？　他说得很不错，进步很快。
你琵琶弹得怎么样？　　　　　　　　　我做得很认真。
你汉字写得好不好？　　　　　　　　　我弹得不怎么样。
你作业做得认真不认真？　　　　　　　他游得很快。
你每天起得早吗？　　　　　　　　　　我汉字写得马马虎虎/还可以。

2.　　　A　　　　　　　　　　　　　　　　　B

你明天几点的飞机？　　　　　　　　　后天上午十二点多到。
你明天几点去机场？　　　　　　　　　谢谢！
飞机飞几个小时？　　　　　　　　　　朋友开车送我去。
你几点到？　　　　　　　　　　　　　下午两点的飞机。
谁送你去？　　　　　　　　　　　　　飞十二个小时。
一路平安！　　　　　　　　　　　　　上午十点半去。

## 第二十三课 Lesson 23

（五）你是 A，请你向 B 提问 Supposing you are A, ask B questions

A：_____?

B：我每天七点半起床。

A：_____?

B：我常常不吃早饭。

A：_____?

B：当然很饿。

A：_____?

B：课间休息时喝杯咖啡，吃点儿东西，这样就不饿了。

（六）根据实际情况回答问题 Answer the questions according to the actual situations

1. 你每天几点起床？
2. 起床以后做什么？
3. 上午你几点上课？
4. 上午你有几节课？
5. 下午有没有课？
6. 不上课的时候你做什么？

（七）跟同学一起完成并练习下列会话 Complete and practice the following conversations with your classmates

（A 在机场接 B）

A：请问，你是从_____来的_____先生吗？

B：是，我是_____。

A：您好！我_____，是来接您的。

B：啊，是吗？太感谢你了。

A：_____先生，您汉语说得真好。

B：哪里，哪里。您过奖了。

A：您汉语是在哪儿学的？

B：我不是在学校学的，是自学的。

A：是吗？没人教你吗？

B：有啊，我爸爸教我。我爸爸是地道（dìdao, genuine）的中国人。

A：是吗？

B：是呀！我爸爸原来是_____大学的学生，我妈妈是_____的留学生，他们在大学认识的。后来，他们结了婚。我是中_____混血儿（hùnxuè'ér, person of mixed blood）。

A：难怪你汉语说得这么好。

B：哪里！

（八）和同学一起表演课文 Act out the text with your classmates

（九）读后说 Read the passage and say it

## 我的一天

我每天早上六点半起床。起床后，先去卫生间刷牙、洗脸，七点吃早饭。吃完早饭，我休息一会儿，预习预习生词、语法和课文，八点去教室上课。现在我们有四门课：综合课、口语课、阅读课和听力课。我们每天上午都有四节课，中午十二点下课后，我去食堂吃午饭。

午饭后我休息一会儿。星期二、星期四下午有课，我去教室上课；星期一、星期三、星期五下午没有课，我去书法班学习书法，还跟老师学弹琵琶。下午四点以后，我去锻炼身体：有时候游泳，有时候跑步或打太极拳。因为坚持锻炼，所以我的身体很好。

晚上我七点吃晚饭。晚饭后，我有时候跟朋友聊一会儿天儿，有时候上一会儿网，有时候跟爸爸妈妈或者朋友视频。

八点以后，我常常学习两三个小时：做练习、复习旧课、预习新课、听录音、读课文、记生词、写汉字。学完后，我先去洗澡，然后上床，睡觉。

来中国后，我每天都很忙，每天都很愉快。

# 第二十三课 Lesson 23

（十）怎么表达 How to express

> dùnwù
> 顿悟　a sudden enlightenment

1. A：Wǒ měi zhōu zuò yí cì jiànměicāo.
   我 每 周 做 一 次 健美操。
   I do aerobics every week.

   B：Guàibude nǐ zhème miáotiao.
   怪不得 你 这么 苗条。
   No wonder you have such a slight figure.

2. A：Tā māma shì Zhōngguórén.
   她 妈妈 是 中国人。
   Her mother is Chinese.

   B：Shì ma? Nánguài tā Hànyǔ shuōde nàme hǎo.
   是 吗？难怪 她 汉语 说得 那么 好。
   Really? No wonder she speaks Chinese so well.

（十一）朗读中国经典诗词，请注意语音语调 Read aloud the classic Chinese poem and pay attention to the pronunciation and intonation.

Zá Shī
## 杂 诗

[Jìn] Táo Yuānmíng
[晋] 陶　渊明　（365—427）

Shèng nián bù chóng lái,　yí rì nán zài chén,
盛 年 不 重 来，一日 难 再 晨，
Jíshí dāng miǎnlì,　suìyuè bú dài rén.
及时 当 勉励，岁月 不 待 人。

（十二）请欣赏下列著名的词句 Please enjoy the following famous saying

Jūnzǐ chéngrénzhīměi.
君子 成人之美。
A gentleman is always ready to help others attain their goals.

# 第二十四课 你在做什么呢
## Dì-èrshísì kè  Nǐ zài zuò shénme ne
### Lesson 24  What are you doing

## 一 课文 Text

（一）你在做什么呢

A：你在做什么呢？
Nǐ zài zuò shénme ne?

B：我在玩儿游戏呢。
Wǒ zài wánr yóuxì ne.

A：好玩儿吗？
Hǎowánr ma?

B：特好玩儿。
Tè hǎowánr.

A：你看几点了？
Nǐ kàn jǐ diǎn le?

B：啊，都七点三刻了。
À, dōu qī diǎn sān kè le.

A：我们该去教室上课了。
Wǒmen gāi qù jiàoshì shàng kè le.

B：糟糕！我还没洗脸呢。
Zāogāo! Wǒ hái méi xǐ liǎn ne.

---

What are you doing

A: What are you doing?
B: I'm playing a game.
A: Is it fun?
B: Yes, it really is.
A: What time do you think it is?

B: Oh, it's a quarter to eight already.
A: It's time for us to go to the classroom.
B: Oh, no! I haven't washed my face yet.

## （二）他们在做什么呢

（爱德华和马丁在用手机里的照片和视频练习说汉语）

Àidéhuá: Nǐ kànzhe wǒ shǒujī li de zhàopiàn hé shìpín, huídá wǒ de wèntí hǎo ma?
爱德华：你看着我手机里的照片和视频，回答我的问题好吗？

Mǎdīng: Nǐ shì ràng wǒ kànzhe zhèxiē liànxí shuō Hànyǔ, duì ma?
马丁：你是让我看着这些练习说汉语，对吗？

Àidéhuá: Nǐ zhēn cōngmíng. Kàn! Tā zài zuò shénme ne?
爱德华：你真聪明。看！他在做什么呢？

Mǎdīng: Tā zài chuān yīfu、 dài màozi、 dài yǎnjìng ne.
马丁：他在穿衣服、戴帽子、戴眼镜呢。

Àidéhuá: Tā ne? Tā zhèng zuò shénme ne?
爱德华：她呢？她正做什么呢？

Mǎdīng: À, tā shì shéi ya? Zhēn piàoliang a.
马丁：啊，她是谁呀？真漂亮啊。

Àidéhuá: Nǐ yào kuài diǎnr yòng Hànyǔ shuō!
爱德华：你要快点儿用汉语说！

Mǎdīng: Tā shì bu shì zhèng huà zhuāng ne?
马丁：她是不是正化妆呢？

Àidéhuá: Zài kàn! Tāmen zhèngzài zuò shénme ne? Yídìng yào kuài diǎnr shuō!
爱德华：再看！他们正在做什么呢？一定要快点儿说！

Mǎdīng: À, tāmen zài dǎ lánqiú、 tī zúqiú、 dǎ wǎngqiú、 dǎ pīngpāngqiú、 pāo zhào、 kū、 xiào…… wǒ bù shuō le, tài lèi le.
马丁：啊，他们在打篮球、踢足球、打网球、打乒乓球、拍照、哭、笑……我不说了，太累了。

Àidéhuá: Zhēn jiāoqì!
爱德华：真娇气！

---

What are they doing

(Edward and Martin are practicing speaking Chinese using photos and videos on Edward's phone)

Edward: Can you look at the photos and videos on my phone and answer my questions?

Martin: You're asking me to look at them to practice speaking Chinese, right?

Edward: You are so clever. Look, what is he doing?

Martin: He's getting dressed and putting on his hat and glasses.

Edward: What about her? What is she doing?

Martin: Oh, who is she? She is really beautiful.

Edward: You must speak quickly in Chinese!

Martin: Is she putting on her make-up?

Edward: Keep looking! What are they doing? You have to speak quickly!

Martin: Ah, they are playing basketball, football, tennis, table tennis, taking pictures, crying, laughing ... I can't do it any more. I'm too tired.

Edward: How vulnerable!

## 二 生词 New Words

| | | | | |
|---|---|---|---|---|
| 1 | 游戏 | yóuxì | 名、动 | game; to play a game |
| 2 | 好玩儿 | hǎowánr | 形 | amusing; fun |
| 3 | 都 | dōu | 副 | already |
| 4 | 刻 | kè | 量 | quarter |
| 5 | 该 | gāi | 助动 | should; ought to |
| 6 | 糟糕 | zāogāo | 形 | bad; terrible |
| 7 | 着 | zhe | 助 | *indicating the continuation of an action or a state* |
| 8 | 聪明 | cōngmíng | 形 | clever; smart |
| 9 | 在 | zài | 副 | *indicating an action in progress* |
| 10 | 衣服 | yīfu | 名 | clothes |
| 11 | 戴 | dài | 动 | to adorn; to wear (accessories) |
| 12 | 帽子 | màozi | 名 | cap; hat |
| 13 | 眼镜 | yǎnjìng | 名 | glasses |
| 14 | 漂亮 | piàoliang | 形 | pretty; beautiful |

| 15 | 化妆 | huà zhuāng | 动 | to put on make-up |
| 16 | 正在 | zhèngzài | 副 | in the process of; in the course of |
| 17 | 打 | dǎ | 动 | to play |
| 18 | 篮球 | lánqiú | 名 | basketball |
| 19 | 踢 | tī | 动 | to kick |
| 20 | 足球 | zúqiú | 名 | football; soccer |
| 21 | 网球 | wǎngqiú | 名 | tennis |
| 22 | 乒乓球 | pīngpāngqiú | 名 | ping-pong; table tennis |
| 23 | 哭 | kū | 动 | to cry; to weep |
| 24 | 笑 | xiào | 动 | to laugh; to smile |
| 25 | 娇气 | jiāoqì | 形 | delicate; fragile |

## 三 注释 Notes

（一）都七点三刻了，该去教室了。

句中的"都"表示"已经"，例如：

In this sentence, "都" means "already". For example:

1. 都八点了，他还没来呢。

2. 他都二十了，不是小孩子了。

3. 昨晚都十一点，我还在做练习呢。

（二）他们正在做什么呢？

动词前边加上副词"在""正在""正"或句尾加"呢"，表示动作的进行。"在""正在"和"正"也可与"呢"同时使用。例如：

When a verb is preceded by the adverb "在", "正在" or "正", or when the particle "呢" is used at the end of a sentence, it indicates that an action is in progress. "在 / 正在 / 正" can also be used together with "呢". Fox example:

1. A：你在做什么呢？
   B：我在玩儿游戏呢。
2. A：马丁正在做什么呢？
   B：他正在练习说汉语呢。
3. A：她正在做什么呢？
   B：她正化妆呢。

"在"重在表示动作进行的状态。"正"重在表示对应某时间点动作的进行。"正在"兼指二者。

"在" emphasizes the state of an action being in progress. "正" emphasizes the progression of an action at a specific time. "正在" emphasizes both the state and the time.

（三）动词 + 着 Verb + 着

动词后边加动态助词"着"，主要用于表示动作的进行或状态的持续。例如：

If a verb is followed by the aspect particle "着", it indicates the continuation of an action or state. For example:

1. 他等着我们呢。
2. 她们用手机聊着天儿。
3. 你是让我看着这些练习说汉语，对吗？

## 四 练习 Exercises

（一）朗读下列发音相近的词语 Read aloud the following words and expressions with similar pronunciation

| yóuxì | yǒu xì | jiàoshì | jiāo shī |
| 游戏 | 有戏 | 教室 | 教诗 |
| sān kè | sǎnkè | tī qiú | dìqiú |
| 三刻 | 散客 | 踢球 | 地球 |
| cōngmíng | cóngmìng | yīfu | yǐ fù |
| 聪明 | 从命 | 衣服 | 已付 |

## 第二十四课 Lesson 24

（二）替换并朗读 Replace and read aloud

1. A：你在做什么呢？
   B：我<u>玩儿游戏</u>呢。

| 玩儿手机 | 发短信 | 拍视频 |
| 化妆 | 做练习 | 洗衣服 |

2. A：他们正在做什么呢？
   B：他们正在<u>打球</u>呢。

| 上课 | 聊天儿 | 踢足球 |
| 打篮球 | 唱歌儿 | 跳舞 |

（三）选词填空并朗读下列句子 Choose the appropriate words to fill in the blanks and read aloud the following sentences

| 该　　特　　没　　玩儿　　看 |

1. A：你在做什么呢？
   B：我在_____游戏呢。
2. A：好玩儿吗？
   B：_____好玩儿。
3. A：你_____几点了？
   B：啊，都七点三刻了。
4. 我们_____去教室上课了。
5. 糟糕！我还_____洗脸呢。

| 不　　快　　让　　回答　　踢　　穿 |

1. 你看着我手机里的照片和视频，_____我的问题，好吗？
2. 你是_____我看着这些照片和视频练习说汉语，对吗？
3. A：对，你很聪明。看，他在做什么呢？
   B：他在_____衣服、戴帽子呢。
4. 你要_____点儿用汉语说！

5. 她是_____是在化妆呢?

6. A：再看！他们正在做什么呢?

   B：啊，他们在打篮球、_____足球、打网球、拍照、打乒乓球、哭、笑……

（四）将 A、B 两列连线，组成正确的句子或对话，然后朗读 Match A with B to make sentences or dialogues and then read the sentences or dialogues aloud

1. 该……了

| A | B |
|---|---|
| 早上六点半了， | 该去教室上课了。 |
| 早上七点了， | 该去上书画课了。 |
| 早上七点三刻了， | 该睡觉了。 |
| 下午四点了， | 我该去爬山了。 |
| 晚上十点半了， | 该去操场打篮球了。 |
| 又到周六了， | 该吃早饭了。 |
| 又到星期日了， | 该起床了。 |

2. 在 / 正在……呢

| A | B |
|---|---|
| 你在做什么呢? | 安丽跟姐姐视频聊天儿呢。 |
| 昨晚七点你在做什么呢? | 我在看网球比赛（bǐsài, match）呢。 |
| 他们两个在做什么呢? | 她在写作业呢。 |
| 马丁正在做什么呢? | 我在听课文录音呢。 |
| 罗兰在做什么呢? | 他在上网玩儿游戏呢。 |
| 安丽跟谁视频聊天儿呢? | 他们在练习说汉语呢。 |

（五）说说每天这些时间，你在做什么 What are you doing at these times every day

| | |
|---|---|
| 6:30—7:00 | |
| 7:00—8:00 | |
| 8:00/8:30—12:00 | |

## 第二十四课  Lesson 24

| | |
|---|---|
| 12:30—14:00 | |
| 16:00—17:00 | |
| 19:00—21:00 | |

（六）你是 B，根据所给的词回答 A 的问题 Suppose you are B. Answer A's question using the words and phrases given

A：他 / 她（们）在做什么呢？

B：他 / 她（们）在_____。

| 睡觉 | 刷牙 | 穿衣服 | 洗脸 |
| 吃饭 | 喝茶 | 喝咖啡 | 看书 |
| 听音乐 | 玩儿手机 | 看电视 | 拍照 |
| 踢足球 | 打太极拳 | 游泳 | 爬山 |
| 跳舞 | 跑步 | 哭 | 笑 |

（七）和同学一起表演课文 Act out the text with your classmates

（八）读后说 Read the passage and say it

今天爱德华用他手机里的照片和视频，跟我一起练习口语。因为课文里学的是"在、正和正在"，他就让我快点儿告诉他照片和视频里的人正做什么呢，在做什么呢，或正在做什么呢？

我当然知道照片或视频里的人在做什么，但用汉语我说得很慢也很累。

（九）怎么表达 How to express

hūjiù
呼救　calling for help

Kuài dǎ yāo èr líng.
1. 快 打 120。

Hurry up! Call 120.

Kuài dǎ yāo yāo líng bào jǐng!
2. 快打 110 报警!
Call 110! Call the police!

Zháo huǒ le! Zháo huǒ le!
3. 着火了!着火了!
Fire! Fire!

Jiù mìng a! Jiù mìng a!
4. 救命啊!救命啊!
Help! Help!

（十）朗读中国经典诗词，请注意语音语调 Read aloud the classic Chinese poem and pay attention to the pronunciation and intonation

Zá Shī
**杂 诗**

[Táng] Wáng Wéi
［唐］王　维（701—761）

Jūn zì gùxiāng lái, yīng zhī gùxiāng shì.
君自故乡来，应知故乡事。

Lái rì qǐ chuāng qián, hán méi zhuó huā wèi?
来日绮窗前，寒梅著花未？

（十一）请欣赏下列著名的词句 Please enjoy the following famous saying

Bù jīng yì fān hán chè gǔ, zěn dé méihuā pūbí xiāng.
不经一番寒彻骨，怎得梅花扑鼻香。

Without the piercing chilliness of the snowfall,

how can we get the fragrant whiff of the plum blossoms?

| 9 | 精彩 | jīngcǎi | 形 | wonderful; brilliant; splendid |
| 10 | 旧 | jiù | 形 | old |
| 11 | 充电 | chōng diàn | 动 | to charge (a battery, etc.) |
| 12 | 麻烦 | máfan | 形、动 | troublesome; to bother |
| 13 | 智能 | zhìnéng | 形 | intelligent; smart |
| 14 | 电脑 | diànnǎo | 名 | computer |
| 15 | 电视机 | diànshìjī | 名 | television |
| 16 | 钟表 | zhōngbiǎo | 名 | clock and watch |
| 17 | 导航仪 | dǎohángyí | 名 | navigator |
| 18 | 照相机 | zhàoxiàngjī | 名 | camera |
| 19 | 气象台 | qìxiàngtái | 名 | meterological observatory |
| 20 | 计算器 | jìsuànqì | 名 | calculator |
| 21 | 指南针 | zhǐnánzhēn | 名 | compass |
| 22 | 日历 | rìlì | 名 | calendar |
| 23 | 总之 | zǒngzhī | 连 | in a word; all in all |
| 24 | 干 | gàn | 动 | to do |

**专名 Zhuānmíng  Proper Noun**

| 吉米 | Jímǐ | | | Jimmy |

## 三 注释 Notes

（一）现在干什么都不能没有手机呀。

"干什么"意思是：做任何事情。

"干什么" means "to do anything".

（二）……是指南针，还是日历，……

这个"还"是副词，表示补充。例如：

The word "还" is an adverb, indicating to complement something. For example.

1. 他学汉语，还学书法。
2. 我想学太极拳，还想学太极剑。

（三）不能没有手机呀。

双重否定，表示肯定，比一般的肯定句语气更强。"不能""没有"都是否定词，加在一起意思是：一定要有。

This is a double negation indicating stronger affirmation. "不能" and "没有" are both negative words. When used together, they mean "must have".

（四）那你还不快点儿去买个新的。

句中的"还"是仍然的意思。用于反问，含有轻微责怪的语气。意思是：你应该快点儿去买个新的。

The word "还" in the sentence means "still". It is used in rhetorical questions, containing a slight tone of blame. This sentence means: "You should go and buy a new one soon."

## 四 练习 Exercises

（一）朗读 Read aloud

1. 朗读下列发音相近的词语 Read aloud the following words and expressions with similar pronunciation

| fēicháng | fēixiáng | gōngnéng | gōngchéng |
| 非常 | 飞翔 | 功能 | 工程 |
| sùdù | sù dú | jiǎnzhí | jiānzhí |
| 速度 | 速读 | 简直 | 兼职 |
| jīngcǎi | jìngcāi | qíquán | qìquán |
| 精彩 | 竞猜 | 齐全 | 弃权 |

## 2. 朗读下列词组 Read the following phrases aloud

| 真漂亮 | 真好用 | 真精彩 | 功能真全 |
| 太麻烦了 | 太便宜了 | 太简单了 | 太好看了 |
| 简直没法儿活 | 简直没法儿说 | 简直没法儿用 | |
| 还不快点儿买 | 还不快点儿走 | 还不快点儿复习 | |

## 3. 朗读下列顺口溜 Read the following doggerel aloud

Shǒujī hé hùzhào,
手机和护照，
Your mobile phone and passport,

qiānwàn bǎoguǎn hǎo.
千万 保管 好。
You must keep them well.

Zǒubiàn quán Zhōngguó,
走遍 全 中国，
All across China,

shíkè lí bu liǎo.
时刻离不了。
You can't go a minute without them.

## （二）替换并朗读 Replace and read aloud

1. A：你的<u>手机</u>是不是新的？
   B：是，我刚买的。

| 词典 | 电脑 | 琵琶 |
| 箱子 | 电动车 | |

2. A：你看，这个手机是谁的？
   B：可能是<u>马丁</u>的。

| 松山 | 李大同 |
| 我同屋 | 老师 |

3. A：你去不去<u>教室</u>？
   B：去。

| 公园 | 图书馆 | 水果店 |
| 我那儿 | 公寓楼 | |

4. A：你买苹果还是买橘子？
   B：我买橘子。

> 买猕猴桃　　买葡萄
> 喝茶　　　　喝咖啡
> 吃馒头　　　吃包子
> 学英语　　　学汉语
> 去银行　　　去图书馆

（提示：生词请查阅各类词典。）

(Tip: For new words, please refer to various dictionaries.)

（三）选词填空并朗读下列句子 Choose the appropriate words to fill in the blanks and read aloud the following sentences

> 的　　还　　刚　　简直　　干　　特别

1. A：你的手机是不是新的？
   B：是，这是我_____买的，你看怎么样？
2. 这个手机非常好用，功能齐全，速度特快。你是不是也想买个新_____？
3. 我这个旧手机不太好用，充电也_____慢，看你用新手机，我也想买个新的。
4. 现在_____什么都不能没有手机呀。
5. 是的，没有手机_____没法儿活。
6. 那你_____不快点儿去买个新的。

（四）你是A，请你向B提问 Supposing you are A, ask B questions

1. A：_____？
   B：我的手机是刚买的。
   A：_____？
   B：非常好用，功能齐全，速度也特快。

2. A：_____？

　　B：我这个旧手机不好用，充电特别慢。

　　A：_____？

　　B：是，我看你用新手机，也想买个新的。

（五）练习提问 Practice asking questions

1. 用"动词＋不＋动词"提问 Ask questions using "verb＋不＋verb"

（1）A：_____？

　　B：我很想去中国。

（2）A：_____？

　　B：我不想吃蛋糕。

（3）A：_____？

　　B：我不喜欢这种颜色。

（4）A：_____？

　　B：我愿意和你一起去。

（5）A：_____？

　　B：这些照片我都可以发给你。

（6）A：_____？

　　B：我不知道这个句子的意思。

2. 用"形容词＋不＋形容词"提问 Ask questions using "adjective＋不＋adjective"

（1）A：_____？

　　B：新课的生词不太多。

（2）A：_____？

　　B：我有点儿累。

（3）A：_____？

　　B：我们班的同学都很努力。

（4）A：_____？

　　B：这个手机不贵。

（5）A：_____？

B：学校离地铁站（dìtiězhàn, subway station）不远。

（6）A：_____？

B：他的个子很高。

（7）A：_____？

B：我写汉字写得不快。

（六）根据实际情况回答问题 Answer the questions according to the actual situations

1. 你的手机是不是新的？
2. 你的手机好用不好用？
3. 你的手机充电快不快？
4. 你每天玩儿手机的时间长不长？
5. 你用不用手机学习汉语？
6. 请说说你都用手机做什么？

（七）和同学一起表演课文 Act out the text with your classmates

（八）读后说 Read the passage and say it

你看，这是我刚买的新手机。怎么样？漂亮吧？它的功能特齐全，速度也非常快。我原来的那个手机不太好用，充电也慢。朋友说："快去买个新的吧！手机不好用太麻烦，现在干什么都不能没有手机。"真的，没有手机简直没法儿活。

（九）怎么表达 How to express

cuīcù
催促　urging sb.; asking sb. to hurry

Kuài diǎnr!　Kuài diǎnr!　Yào chídào le.
1. 快 点儿！快 点儿！要 迟到 了。
Hurry up! Hurry up! We'll be late.

2. A：<ruby>啊<rt>À</rt></ruby>，<ruby>都<rt>dōu</rt></ruby> <ruby>七点<rt>qī diǎn</rt></ruby> <ruby>了<rt>le</rt></ruby>。

   Ah, it's already seven o'clock.

   B：<ruby>那<rt>Nà</rt></ruby> <ruby>你<rt>nǐ</rt></ruby> <ruby>还<rt>hái</rt></ruby> <ruby>不<rt>bú</rt></ruby> <ruby>快点儿<rt>kuài diǎnr</rt></ruby> <ruby>起<rt>qǐ</rt></ruby> <ruby>床<rt>chuáng</rt></ruby>？

   Why don't you get up at once?

3. <ruby>别<rt>Bié</rt></ruby> <ruby>磨蹭<rt>móceng</rt></ruby> <ruby>了<rt>le</rt></ruby>，<ruby>快<rt>kuài</rt></ruby> <ruby>走<rt>zǒu</rt></ruby> <ruby>吧<rt>ba</rt></ruby>。

   Stop dawdling and get going.

（十）朗读中国经典诗词，请注意语音语调 Read aloud the classic Chinese poem and pay attention to the pronunciation and intonation

### 赠 花卿
*Zèng Huāqīng*

［唐］杜甫（712—770）
*[Táng] Dù Fǔ*

锦城 丝管日纷纷，半入江风半入云。
*Jǐnchéng sī guǎn rì fēnfēn, bàn rù jiāng fēng bàn rù yún.*

此曲只应 天上 有，人间 能 得几回闻？
*Cǐ qǔ zhǐ yīng tiānshang yǒu, rénjiān néng dé jǐ huí wén?*

（十一）请欣赏下列著名的词句 Please enjoy the following famous saying

人 贵 有 自知之明。
*Rén guì yǒu zìzhīzhīmíng.*

To know one's own limitation is of great importance.

# 第二十六课 刚才我跑步了
## Lesson 26 — I went running just now
### Dì-èrshíliù kè  Gāngcái wǒ pǎo bù le

## 一 课文 Text

（早晨，丹尼斯在操场上碰到了爱德华）

Dānnísī: Hēi, nǐ hǎo, Àidéhuá.
丹尼斯：嘿，你好，爱德华。

Àidéhuá: Nǐ hǎo, Dānnísī.
爱德华：你好，丹尼斯。

Dānnísī: Nǐ gāngcái shì bu shì pǎo bù le?
丹尼斯：你刚才是不是跑步了？

Àidéhuá: Shì, nǐ kàn, pǎode mǎn tóu dà hàn. Nǐ zuò shénme yùndòng le?
爱德华：是，你看，跑得满头大汗。你做什么运动了？

Dānnísī: Wǒ gāng xuéwán tàijíquán. Nǐ měi tiān dōu duànliàn ma?
丹尼斯：我刚学完太极拳。你每天都锻炼吗？

Àidéhuá: Shì, wǒ tiāntiān dōu duànliàn.
爱德华：是，我天天都锻炼。

Dānnísī: Nǐ xǐhuan shénme yùndòng?
丹尼斯：你喜欢什么运动？

Àidéhuá: Zài guó nèi shí wǒ xǐhuan zúqiú hé yóu yǒng; lái Zhōngguó yǐhòu, wǒ mí-shàng le chángpǎo hé wǔshù. Wǒ měi tiān zǎoshang jiānchí rào cāochǎng pǎo shí duō quānr, xiàwǔ gēn wǔshù lǎoshī liàn gōng. Nǐ shì zěnme duànliàn shēntǐ de?
爱德华：在国内时我喜欢足球和游泳；来中国以后，我迷上了长跑和武术。我每天早上坚持绕操场跑十多圈儿，下午跟武术老师练功。你是怎么锻炼身体的？

## 第二十六课 Lesson 26

Dānnísī: Wǒ yī、sān、wǔ zǎoshang gēn lǎoshī xué tàijíquán, èr、sì xiàwǔ
丹尼斯：我一、三、五早上跟老师学太极拳，二、四下午

zuò jiànměicāo, xīngqīliù gēn dēngshānduì yìqǐ qù pá shān.
做健美操，星期六跟登山队一起去爬山。

Àidéhuá: Shì wǒmen xuéxiào de dēngshānduì ma?
爱德华：是我们学校的登山队吗？

Dānnísī: Shì a, shì Zhōngguó tóngxué zǔzhī de, Wú Dān jièshào wǒ cānjiā de.
丹尼斯：是啊，是中国同学组织的，吴丹介绍我参加的。

Àidéhuá: Měi xīngqīliù dōu qù ma?
爱德华：每星期六都去吗？

Dānnísī: Duì, měi zhōuliù dōu qù pá, bùguǎn guā fēng háishi xià yǔ.
丹尼斯：对，每周六都去爬，不管刮风还是下雨。

Àidéhuá: Láihuí xūyào duō cháng shíjiān?
爱德华：来回需要多长时间？

Dānnísī: Bàntiān ba, wǒmen zǎoshang chūfā, xiàwǔ huílai.
丹尼斯：半天吧，我们早上出发，下午回来。

Àidéhuá: Nǐmen tài bàng le!
爱德华：你们太棒了！

Dānnísī: Duànliàn shēntǐ yào jiānchí, zhǐyào jiānchí duànliàn, shēntǐ jiù yídìng
丹尼斯：锻炼身体要坚持，只要坚持锻炼，身体就一定

bàng.
棒。

Àidéhuá: Nǐ shuōde duì, shēngmìng zàiyú yùndòng ma.
爱德华：你说得对，生命在于运动嘛。

---

**I went running just now**

(In the morning, Dennis and Edward met on the playground)

Dennis: Hi, Edward.

Edward: Hello, Dennis.

Dennis: Did you just run?

Edward: Yeah, you see, I'm sweating like a pig. What exercise did you do?

Dennis: I've just finished *taijiquan* lesson. Do you exercise every day?

Edward: Yes, I exercise every day.

Dennis: What kind of sports do you like?

Edward: I used to like football and swimming when I was in my country. After coming to China, I became fascinated by long-distance running and martial arts. I run around the playground more than ten laps every morning and practice kung fu with my martial arts teacher in the afternoon. How do you exercise?

Dennis: I learn *taijiquan* from my teacher on Monday, Wednesday and Friday mornings and do aerobics on Tuesday and Thursday afternoons. I climb the mountain with the mountaineering team on Saturday.

Edward: Our university's mountaineering team?

Dennis: Yes, it is organized by Chinese students. Wu Dan introduced me to it.

Edward: Do you go every Saturday?

Dennis: Yes, I go climbing every Saturday, rain or shine.

Edward: How long does the round trip take?

Dennis: It'll take half a day. We leave in the morning and come back in the afternoon.

Edward: You are awesome.

Dennis: What matters for exercise is perseverance. As long as you persevere, your body will be fit.

Edward: You're right.

## 二  生词 New Words

| | | | | |
|---|---|---|---|---|
| 1 | 刚才 | gāngcái | 名 | just now |
| 2 | 跑步 | pǎo bù | 动 | to run |
|  | 跑 | pǎo | 动 | to run |
|  | 步 | bù | 名 | step; pace |
| 3 | 了 | le | 助 | used at the end of a sentence or a pause in the middle of a sentence to indicate a change or new situation |
| 4 | 早晨 | zǎochen | 名 | morning |
| 5 | 操场 | cāochǎng | 名 | playground |
| 6 | 碰 | pèng | 动 | to meet by chance |
| 7 | 嘿 | hēi | 叹 | hi; hey |
| 8 | 满头大汗 | mǎn tóu dà hàn | | to be covered with sweat on one's head |
|  | 满 | mǎn | 形 | full; filled |
|  | 头 | tóu | 名 | head |

· 80 ·

| | 汗 | hàn | 名 | sweat |
|---|---|---|---|---|
| 9 | 运动 | yùndòng | 名、动 | sports; to exercise |
| 10 | 完 | wán | 动 | to be finished; to be over |
| 11 | 太极拳 | tàijíquán | 名 | *taijiquan*, shadowboxing |
| 12 | 锻炼 | duànliàn | 动 | to take exercise; to have physical training |
| 13 | 游泳 | yóu yǒng | 动 | to swim |
| 14 | 迷 | mí | 动 | to be fascinated by |
| 15 | 长跑 | chángpǎo | 名 | long-distance running |
| 16 | 武术 | wǔshù | 名 | martial arts |
| 17 | 圈儿 | quānr | 名、量 | circle; lap |
| 18 | 练功 | liàn gōng | 动 | to practice one's skill |
| 19 | 健美操 | jiànměicāo | 名 | aerobics |
| 20 | 登山队 | dēngshānduì | 名 | mountaineering team |
| | 登山 | dēng shān | 动 | to climb a mountain |
| | 山 | shān | 名 | mountain |
| 21 | 爬山 | pá shān | | to climb a mountain |
| | 爬 | pá | 动 | to climb |
| 22 | 组织 | zǔzhī | 动、名 | to organize; organization |
| 23 | 参加 | cānjiā | 动 | to join; to participate |
| 24 | 刮 | guā | 动 | (of wind) to blow |
| 25 | 风 | fēng | 名 | wind |
| 26 | 来回 | láihuí | 动 | to and fro |
| | 回 | huí | 动 | to return; to come/go back |
| 27 | 需要 | xūyào | 动 | to need |
| 28 | 半天 | bàntiān | | half a day |

| 29 | 出发 | chūfā | 动 | to start off; to depart |
| 30 | 回来 | huílai | 动 | to return; to come back |
| 31 | 只要 | zhǐyào | 连 | as long as; if only |
| 32 | 生命 | shēngmìng | 名 | life |
| 33 | 在于 | zàiyú | 动 | to lie in; to depend on |

## 三 注释 Notes

### （一）语气助词"了" The modal particle "了"

语气助词"了"用在句尾，表示肯定的语气，有成句的作用。说明事情的发生、动作的完成、情况的出现和状态的变化等。例如：

The modal particle "了" is used at the end of a sentence to express the affirmative mood, which has the function of forming a sentence. It explains the occurrence of an event, the completion of an action, the emergence of a situation, and a change in state, etc. For example:

1. 早晨，丹尼斯与爱德华在操场相遇了。
2. 你刚才是不是跑步了？
3. 你做什么运动了？

试比较下列两组句子：

Compare the following two groups of sentences:

| 事情发生前 | 事情发生后 |
|---|---|
| Before the event | After the event |
| A：你去哪儿？ → | A：你去哪儿了？ |
| B：我去操场。 → | B：我去操场了。 |
| A：你做什么？ → | A：你做什么了？ |
| B：我跑步。 → | B：我跑步了。 |

## （二）结果补语 Result complement

动词"完、懂、见、开、上、到、给、成"和形容词"好、对、错、熟、早、晚"等都可以放在动词后边做结果补语，表示动作行为的结果。例如：

The verbs "完, 懂, 见, 开, 上, 到, 给, 成" and the adjectives "好, 对, 错, 熟, 早, 晚", etc., can be placed after a verb as its complement, indicating the result of an action. For example:

1. 我刚学完太极拳。
2. 来中国以后，我迷上了长跑和武术。
3. 老师的话我听懂了。
4. 这个问题我答对了。

## （三）只要 as long as; if only

连词"只要"和"就"或"便"连接一个条件复句。"只要"引出一个必要的条件；"就"（便）后边是这个条件所产生的结果。例如：

"只要……就（便）……" joins the two clauses of a conditional complex sentence. "只要" introduces a necessary condition, and what follows "就"（便）is the result this condition brings about. For example:

1. 锻炼身体要坚持，只要坚持锻炼，身体就一定棒。
2. 你只要努力，就一定能学好。
3. 你只要请他，他便会来。

## 四 练习 Exercises

### （一）朗读下列发音相近的词语 Read aloud the following words and expressions with similar pronunciation

| gāngcái | gàncái | yùndòng | yùnyòng |
| 刚才 | 干才 | 运动 | 运用 |
| wǔshù | wúshù | bùguǎn | bùgān |
| 武术 | 无数 | 不管 | 不甘 |
| zǔzhī | zǔzhǐ | shēngmìng | shēngmíng |
| 组织 | 阻止 | 生命 | 声明 |

（二）替换并朗读 Replace and read aloud

1. 跑得满头大汗。

| 吃 干 热 走 打 累 |

2. 我天天都锻炼。

| 跑步　打太极拳　做健美操 |
| 游泳　练书法　　画画儿 |

3. 来中国以后，我迷上了长跑和武术。

| 太极拳　　汉字书法　做饭 |
| 画山水画儿　中医　　茶道 |

4. A：你喜欢什么运动？
   B：我喜欢游泳。

| 踢足球　打篮球　长跑 |
| 体操　　爬山　　打太极拳 |

5. 只要坚持锻炼，身体就一定棒。

| 天天上课　学习　好 |
| 你去　　　我　　　去 |
| 你努力　　汉语　说得好 |
| 多交朋友　你　　不会感到孤单 |
| 你坚持　　困难　不算什么 |

（三）选词填空并朗读下列句子 Choose the appropriate words to fill in the blanks and read aloud the following sentences

| 喜欢　跟　碰　完　在　得 |

1. 早晨，丹尼斯在操场_____到了爱德华。
2. A：刚才是不是跑步了？
   B：是，你看，我跑_____满头大汗。你做什么运动了？
3. 我刚学_____太极拳。

## 第二十六课 Lesson 26

4. 在国内时我_____足球和游泳；来中国以后，我迷上了长跑和武术。

5. 我每天早上坚持绕操场跑十多圈，下午_____武术老师练功。

爬　就　出发　多　怎么　还是

1. 你_____锻炼身体？
2. 我一、三、五早上跟老师学太极拳，二、四下午做健美操，星期六跟登山队一起去_____山。
3. 不管刮风_____下雨，我们每星期六都去爬山。
4. 来回要_____长时间？
5. 半天吧，我们早上_____，下午回来。
6. 锻炼身体要坚持，只要坚持锻炼，身体_____一定健康。

迷上　看上　吃上　喝上　爱上　喜欢上

1. 我现在已经_____了这里的生活。
2. 我昨天在网上商店_____了一件大衣。
3. 他已经_____了这个专业，觉得越学越有意思（yǒu yìsi, interesting）。
4. 他现在_____了中国武术，天天都练。
5. 没想到，我现在能_____中国菜。
6. 很高兴能_____真正的龙井茶。

（四）你是 A，请你向 B 提问 Supposing you are A, ask B questions

A: _____？
B: 我喜欢跑步。

A: _____？
B: 现在我每天下午去操场跑步。

A: _____？
B: 丹尼斯喜欢爬山。

A：_____？
B：我不太喜欢爬山。
A：_____？
B：太远，也太累。

（五）完成下列句子并大声朗读 Complete the following sentences and read them aloud

1. 只要你想去，我_____。（就）
2. _____，我就一定帮助她。（只要）
3. 只要想见朋友，我_____。（就）
4. 这本词典不管贵还是便宜，_____。（都）
5. 不管汉语多么难学，_____。（都）
6. _____，我每天都锻炼一个小时。（不管）

（六）根据实际情况回答问题 Answer the questions according to the actual situations

1. 你在你们国家的时候，喜欢什么体育运动？
2. 来留学以后，你每天都锻炼身体吗？
3. 你怎么锻炼身体？
4. 你能坚持下去吗？
5. 你学过武术吗？
6. 你会不会打太极拳？不会的话，想学吗？

（七）和同学一起表演课文 Act out the text with your classmates

（八）读后说 Read the passage and say it

　　我今天早上在操场锻炼的时候跟丹尼斯聊天儿。她说她每天都坚持锻炼：一、三、五学打太极拳，二、四练健美操。星期六跟学校的登山队去爬山。爬山来回要半天，她不管是刮风还是下雨都去。

　　我也喜欢锻炼，在国内时我喜欢足球和游泳；来中国以后，我迷上了长跑和武术。因为坚持锻炼，所以我的身体很好，每天都快快乐乐的。

# 第二十六课 Lesson 26

(九) 怎么表达 How to express

| àihào |
| 爱好  hobbies |

1. Nǐ yǒu shénme àihào?
   你有 什么 爱好?
   What are your hobbies?

2. Wǒ kù'ài yùndòng.
   我 酷爱 运动。
   I'm crazy about sports.

3. Wǒ de àihào shì lǚyóu.
   我 的 爱好 是 旅游。
   My hobby is traveling.

(十) 朗读中国经典诗词，请注意语音语调 Read aloud the classic Chinese poem and pay attention to the pronunciation and intonation

Yì Jiāngnán
## 忆 江南

[Táng] Bái jūyì
[唐] 白居易（772—846）

Jiāngnán hǎo, fēngjǐng jiù céng ān.　Rì chū jiāng huā hóng shèng huǒ,
江南 好, 风景 旧 曾 谙。日出 江 花 红 胜 火,

chūn lái jiāng shuǐ lǜ rú lán. Néng bú yì Jiāngnán?
春来 江 水 绿 如 蓝。能 不 忆 江南?

(十一) 请欣赏下列著名的词句 Please enjoy the following famous saying

Rén wǎng gāo chù zǒu, shuǐ wǎng dī chù liú.
人 往 高 处 走, 水 往 低 处 流。
Man struggles upwards; water flows downwards.

# 第二十七课 我要了一碗牛肉面
## Lesson 27  I ordered a bowl of beef noodles

Dì-èrshíqī kè　Wǒ yàole yì wǎn niúròumiàn

## 一 课文 Text

（一）去哪个食堂吃呢

A：你吃了吗？
　　Nǐ chīle ma?

B：还没呢。我正等你一块儿吃呢。
　　Hái méi ne. Wǒ zhèng děng nǐ yíkuàir chī ne.

A：今天咱们去哪个食堂吃呢？
　　Jīntiān zánmen qù nǎge shítáng chī ne?

B：还是去第一食堂吧，那里的饭菜好一些。
　　Háishi qù dì-yī shítáng ba, nàlǐ de fàncài hǎo yìxiē.

A：咱们去第三食堂吧，我听说那儿的牛肉面特别好吃。
　　Zánmen qù dì-sān shítáng ba, wǒ tīngshuō nàr de niúròumiàn tèbié hǎochī.

B：好，走吧。
　　Hǎo, zǒu ba.

---

Which canteen shall we go to

A: Have you eaten?
B: Not yet. I am waiting for you to eat with me.
A: Which canteen shall we go to today?
B: Let's go to the first canteen. The food there is better.
A: Let's go to the third canteen. I've heard the beef noodles there are delicious.
B: All right, let's go.

（二）我要了一碗牛肉面

A：你要的什么？
　　Nǐ yào de shénme?

## 第二十七课 Lesson 27

B: 我要了一碗牛肉面。你呢?
Wǒ yàole yì wǎn niúròumiàn. Nǐ ne?

A: 我吃包子。你想喝点儿什么?
Wǒ chī bāozi. Nǐ xiǎng hē diǎnr shénme?

B: 我喝矿泉水。
Wǒ hē kuàngquánshuǐ.

A: 我喝啤酒。牛肉面的味道怎么样?
Wǒ hē píjiǔ. Niúròumiàn de wèidào zěnmeyàng?

B: 很好吃。你尝尝。
Hěn hǎochī. Nǐ chángchang.

A: 啊,不错。这包子也很好吃。你也吃一个吧。
À, búcuò. Zhè bāozi yě hěn hǎochī. Nǐ yě chī yí gè ba.

B: 谢谢,我已经吃饱了,不能再吃了。
Xièxie, wǒ yǐjīng chībǎo le, bù néng zài chī le.

---

I ordered a bowl of beef noodles

A: What did you order?
B: I ordered a bowl of beef noodles. And you?
A: Steamed stuffed buns. What would you like to drink?
B: I'd like mineral water.
A: I'd like beer. How do the beef noodles taste?
B: Very delicious. Try it.
A: Ah, good. The buns are also very delicious. You can have one, too.
B: Thank you. I've had enough. I can't eat any more.

## 二 生词 New Words

| | | | | |
|---|---|---|---|---|
| 1 | 要 | yào | 动 | to order; to buy; to ask for |
| 2 | 了 | le | 助 | used after a verb or an adjective to indicate the completion of an action or a change |
| 3 | 碗 | wǎn | 名 | bowl |
| 4 | 牛肉面 | niúròumiàn | 名 | beef noodles |
| 5 | 面 | miàn | 名 | noodles; flour |
| 6 | 等 | děng | 动 | to wait |

| 7 | 一块儿 | yíkuàir | 副 | together |
| --- | --- | --- | --- | --- |
| 8 | 食堂 | shítáng | 名 | dining hall; canteen |
| 9 | 第 | dì | 词头 | *used before numerals to form ordinal numbers* 第三食堂 |
| 10 | 饭 | fàn | 名 | meal; food |
| 11 | 菜 | cài | 名 | dishes; greens |
| 12 | 矿泉水 | kuàngquánshuǐ | 名 | mineral water |
| 13 | 啤酒 | píjiǔ | 名 | beer |
| 14 | 味道 | wèidào | 名 | taste |
| 15 | 错 | cuò | 形 | bad; poor (used in the negative: 不错 not bad) |
| 16 | 已经 | yǐjīng | 副 | already |
| 17 | 饱 | bǎo | 形 | full |
| 18 | 再 | zài | 副 | once more; again |

## 三　注释 Notes

（一）"动词 + 了""Verb + 了"

动词后边加上动态助词"了"表示动作完成。比较：

A verb followed by the aspect particle "了" indicates the completion of an action. Compare:

    无"了"　　　　　　有"了"

    A：你喝吗？　　　　A：你喝了吗？

    B：我喝。　　　　　B：我喝了。

    A：他喝吗？　　　　A：他喝了吗？

    B：他不喝。　　　　B：他没（有）喝。

(二)"动词 + 了 + 宾语" "Verb + 了 + object"

"动词 + 了"带宾语时,宾语前要有数量词或其他词语做定语。例如:

If "verb + 了" takes an object, a numeral-measure compound or some other word is required before the object as its attribute. For example:

(1) 我要了<u>一碗</u>牛肉面。

(2) 他喝了<u>一瓶</u>啤酒。

(3) 我吃了<u>一个</u>包子。

注意:以上句子,如果没有数量词或定语,语气不完整,不能成句。

Note: If there is no numeral-measure compound or attribute in the above sentences, the mood will not be complete, and the sentences will not valid.

不能只说:*我吃了牛肉面。

要说:我吃了牛肉面,觉得味道不错。

## 四 练习 Exercises

(一) 朗读下列发音相近的词语 Read aloud the following words and expressions with similar pronunciation

| shítáng | chítáng | yì wǎn | yí wàn |
| 食堂 | 池塘 | 一碗 | 一万 |
| wèidào | wēitiáo | chángchang | chàngchang |
| 味道 | 微调 | 尝尝 | 唱唱 |
| bǎo le | hǎo le | shǎo le | zǎo le |
| 饱了 | 好了 | 少了 | 早了 |

(二) 替换并朗读 Replace and read aloud

1. A：你要的什么？
   B：我要了<u>一碗</u> <u>牛肉面</u>。

| | |
|---|---|
| 两个 | 包子 |
| 一碗 | 炸酱面 |
| 一个 | 比萨 |
| 一碗 | 蛋炒饭 |
| 十个 | 饺子 |
| 一个 | 馒头 |

2. A：你想喝点儿什么？
   B：我想喝<u>啤酒</u>。

矿泉水　酸奶　果汁
牛奶　红茶　绿茶　可乐

3. 我已经吃<u>饱</u>了，<u>不能再吃</u>了。

| | |
|---|---|
| 喝好 | 不能再喝 |
| 去过 | 不能再去 |
| 看过 | 不想再看 |
| 玩儿过 | 不想再玩儿 |
| 听过 | 不想再听 |
| 买 | 不能再买 |

## 小词典

| | | | | |
|---|---|---|---|---|
| 1 | 炸酱面 | zhájiàngmiàn | 名 | noodles with soybean paste |
| 2 | 比萨 | bǐsà | 名 | pizza |
| 3 | 蛋炒饭 | dànchǎofàn | 名 | fried rice with egg |
| 4 | 酸奶 | suānnǎi | 名 | yogurt |
| 5 | 果汁 | guǒzhī | 名 | juice |
| 6 | 牛奶 | niúnǎi | 名 | milk |

# 第二十七课 Lesson 27

（三）选词填空并朗读下列句子 Choose the appropriate words to fill in the blanks and read aloud the following sentences

碗　一块儿　饱　味道　特别　一些

1. A：你吃了吗？还没呢。
   B：我正等你_____吃呢。
2. A：今天咱们去哪个食堂吃呢？
   B：还是去第一食堂吧，那里的饭菜好_____。
3. 咱们去第三食堂吧，我听说那儿的牛肉面_____好吃。
4. A：你要的什么？
   B：我要了一_____牛肉面。
5. A：牛肉面的_____怎么样？
   B：很好吃，你尝尝。
6. A：这包子也很好吃，你也吃一个吧。
   B：谢谢，我已经吃_____了，不能再吃了。

（四）你是A，请你向B提问 Supposing you are A, ask B questions

1. A：_____？
   B：我还没吃饭。
2. A：_____？
   B：我去食堂吃午饭。
3. A：_____？
   B：我吃包子。
4. A：_____？
   B：我吃了三个包子。
5. A：_____？
   B：包子很好吃。
6. A：_____？
   B：我喝了啤酒。

（五）完成下列会话并大声朗读 Complete the following conversation and read it aloud

A：你买的什么？
B：_____，你呢？
A：我吃包子。牛肉面好吃吗？
B：_____。
A：不错。包子也很好吃，你尝尝。
B：_____。

（六）和同学一起表演课文 Act out the text with your classmates

（七）读后说 Read the passage and say it

中午我和麦克去第三食堂吃午饭。这个食堂很大，也很好。我买的牛肉面很好吃，麦克尝了尝也说好吃。他说他买的包子也很好吃，要我也吃一个。我说我吃饱了，不能再吃了。

（八）怎么表达 How to express

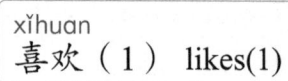

Nǐ zuì xǐhuan de kè shì shénme?
1. A：你 最 喜欢 的课是 什么？
   What's your favorite class?

   Wǒ xiǎng shì kǒuyǔ kè.
   B：我 想 是 口语课。
   I think it's spoken Chinese class.

Wǒ zuì xǐhuan de shì yóu yǒng.
2. 我 最喜欢 的是 游 泳。
   I like swimming the best.

Wǒ xǐhuan cānguān bówùguǎn、kàn diànyǐng、shàng wǎng mǎi dōngxi.
3. 我 喜欢 参观 博物馆、看 电影、上 网 买东西。
   I like visiting museums, going to the cinema and shopping online.

(九) 朗读中国经典诗词，请注意语音语调 Read aloud the classic Chinese poem and pay attention to the pronunciation and intonation

Huí Xiāng Ǒu Shū
**回 乡 偶 书**

[Táng] Hè Zhīzhāng
［唐］贺　知章（659— 744）

Shào xiǎo lí jiā lǎo dà huí, xiāng yīn wú gǎi bìnmáo shuāi.
少 小 离 家 老 大 回，乡 音 无 改 鬓毛 衰。

Értóng xiāngjiàn bù xiāngshí, xiào wèn kè cóng hé chù lái.
儿童 相见 不 相识，笑 问 客 从 何 处来。

(十) 请欣赏下列著名的词句 Please enjoy the following famous saying

Ér xíng qiān lǐ mǔ dānyōu.
儿 行 千里母 担忧。

A mother always worries about her traveling child.

# 第二十八课 我常去超市买东西
## Dì-èrshíbā kè  Wǒ cháng qù chāoshì mǎi dōngxi
## Lesson 28  I often go shopping in the supermarket

## 一 课文 Text

### （一）我常去超市买东西

A：Wǒ yào qù chāoshì, nǐ qù bu qù?
我要去超市，你去不去？

B：Wǒ yě xiǎng qù guàngguang, zánmen yìqǐ qù ba.
我也想去逛逛，咱们一起去吧。

A：Chāoshì yīngyǒu-jìnyǒu, gèzhǒng-gèyàng de dōngxi yòu hǎo yòu piányi, suǒyǐ,
超市应有尽有，各种各样的东西又好又便宜，所以，
wǒ cháng qù chāoshì mǎi dōngxi.
我常去超市买东西。

B：Jīntiān nǐ yào mǎi shénme?
今天你要买什么？

A：Wǒ de táidēng huài le, yào mǎi yí ge xīn de, zài mǎi diǎnr chī de. Nǐ ne?
我的台灯坏了，要买一个新的，再买点儿吃的。你呢？

B：Wǒ mǎi zhǐ hé bǐ.
我买纸和笔。

---

I often go shopping in the supermarket

A: I'm going to the supermarket. Are you going?
B: I also want to go to the supermarket. Let's go together.
A: The supermarket has everything, all kinds of good and inexpensive things, so I often go shopping in the supermarket.
B: What are you going to buy today?
A: My lamp is broken. I need a new one and something to eat. What about you?
B: I want to buy paper and pens.

## （二）你都买什么了

（在超市）

A：你看我买的，一个台灯、一包花生、一盒巧克力、一瓶果酱……

B：真不少。

A：你都买什么了？

B：因为星期三我要上书画课，所以买了两支毛笔、一瓶墨汁和几张宣纸。

A：去结账吧。我刷卡，你呢？

B：我用微信支付。

---

What did you buy

(At the supermarket)

A: Look! I bought a lamp, a bag of peanuts, a box of chocolate, a bottle of jam...

B: You bought quite a lot.

A: What did you buy?

B: Because I have a painting and calligraphy class on Wednesday, I bought two writing brushes, a bottle of ink and some rice paper.

A: Let's go to pay. I'll pay by credit card, and you?

B: I'll pay with WeChat.

## 二 生词 New Words

| | | | | |
|---|---|---|---|---|
| 1 | 超市 | chāoshì | 名 | supermarket |
| 2 | 东西 | dōngxi | 名 | thing; stuff |
| 3 | 逛 | guàng | 动 | to stroll; to roam |

| 4 | 应有尽有 | yīngyǒu-jìnyǒu | | to have everything that one expects to find |
|---|---|---|---|---|
| 5 | 各种各样 | gèzhǒng-gèyàng | | all kinds of |
| 6 | 又 | yòu | 副 | and also; as well as |
| 7 | 所以 | suǒyǐ | 连 | therefore; so |
| 8 | 台灯 | táidēng | 名 | table lamp |
| 9 | 坏 | huài | 形 | bad; broken |
| 10 | 包 | bāo | 量、名 | bag; package; bundle |
| 11 | 花生 | huāshēng | 名 | peanut |
| 12 | 盒 | hé | 量、名 | box |
| 13 | 巧克力 | qiǎokèlì | 名 | chocolate |
| 14 | 瓶 | píng | 量、名 | bottle |
| 15 | 果酱 | guǒjiàng | 名 | jam |
| 16 | 因为 | yīnwèi | 连 | because |
| 17 | 支 | zhī | 量 | *a measure word for pens, pencils, etc.* |
| 18 | 毛笔 | máobǐ | 名 | writing brush |
| 19 | 墨汁 | mòzhī | 名 | prepared Chinese ink |
| 20 | 宣纸 | xuānzhǐ | 名 | rice paper; *xuan* paper |
| 21 | 结账 | jié zhàng | 动 | to settle accounts; to pay the bill |
| 22 | 刷卡 | shuā kǎ | 动 | to swipe a card |
| 23 | 支付 | zhīfù | 动 | to pay |

## 第二十八课 Lesson 28

### 三 注释 Notes

**（一）因为……所以…… because... (so/therefore...)**

"因为……所以……"连接一个因果复句，表达事情的原因和结果。例如：

"因为……所以……" joins the two clauses of a cause-effect complex sentence and indicates the cause and effect of something. For example:

1. 因为要上书画课，所以我要买毛笔和墨汁。
2. 因为我要在中国四年，所以办了个活期账户。
3. 因为我的台灯坏了，所以买了个新的。

"因为"和"所以"都可以单独使用，"因为"表示原因，"所以"表示结果。例如：

"因为" and "所以" can be used separately. "因为" tells the cause, and "所以" tells the effect. For example:

1. 因为两位老人对我很好，我很快乐。
2. 我觉得很寂寞（jìmò, lonely），所以常常想回国（huí guó, to return to one's country）。

**（二）又……又…… both... and...**

"又……又……"用来连接并列的形容词或形容词词组、动词或动词词组，表达两种情况或两种状态同时存在。例如：

"又……又……" is used to connect coordinate adjectives, verbs or verbal or adjectival phrases to denote the simultaneous existence of two situations or states. For example:

1. 这件衣服又好看又便宜。
2. 超市的东西又好又便宜。
3. 这些苹果又大又甜。

**（三）概数的表达 Expressing approximate numbers**

汉语可以用"几""多"表达概数。

"几" and "多" can be used to express approximate numbers in Chinese.

1. "几"一般表示十以下的概数。

"几" usually indicates an approximate number which is smaller than 10.

例如：For example:

（1）我买了几张宣纸。

（2）再来一些草莓和几个猕猴桃吧。

2. "多"用在数量词后，表示不确定的零数。

"多" is used after a numeral-measure compound to indicate a fractional amount which is uncertain.

例如：For example:

（1）这些葡萄有一斤多。

（2）这双鞋四百多块。

（3）我来中国三个多月了。

## 四 练习 Exercises

（一）朗读下列发音相近的词语 Read aloud the following words and expressions with similar pronunciation

| chāoshì | chāoshí | dōngxi | dōng xī |
|---|---|---|---|
| 超市 | 超时 | 东西 | 东 西 |
| yìqǐ | yìqi | piányi | biànlì |
| 一起 | 义气 | 便宜 | 便利 |
| huài le | bài le | mǎile | màile |
| 坏了 | 败了 | 买了 | 卖了 |

（二）替换并朗读 Replace and read aloud

1. <u>超市</u>的<u>东西</u>又<u>好</u>又<u>便宜</u>。

| 食堂的菜 | 便宜 | 好吃 |
|---|---|---|
| 我们的教室 | 干净 | 明亮 |
| 这种苹果 | 大 | 甜 |
| 我现在 | 累 | 渴 |
| 我每天 | 忙 | 快乐 |

2. 因为星期三我要上书法课，所以要买毛笔和墨汁。

| | |
|---|---|
| 超市的东西 | 我常常去超市 |
| 又好又便宜 | 买东西 |
| 我女朋友是中国人 | 我来中国学汉语 |
| 我又学汉语又学书法 | 每天都很忙 |
| 我喜欢学习汉语 | 每天都很快乐 |
| 他病了 | 昨天没来上课 |
| 路上车太多了 | 我不喜欢开车 |

（三）选词填空并朗读下列句子 Choose the appropriate words to fill in the blanks and read aloud the following sentences

所以　支　个　一起　常　包

1. A：我要去超市，你去不去？
   B：我也想去超市逛逛，咱们_____去吧。

2. 超市应有尽有，各种各样的东西又好又便宜，所以，我_____去超市买东西。

3. A：今天你要买什么？
   B：我的台灯坏了，要买一_____新的。

4. 你看我买的，一个台灯、一_____花生、一盒巧克力、一瓶果酱……

5. 因为星期三我要上书画课，_____买了两_____毛笔、一瓶墨汁和几张宣纸。

(四) 完成下列会话并大声朗读 Complete the following conversation and read it aloud

A：我要去超市，你去不去？
B：_____。
A：你常去超市买东西吗？
B：_____。
A：你今天要买什么？
B：_____。
A：你为什么买毛笔和墨汁？
B：_____。
A：你都买什么了？
B：_____。

(五) 将A、B两列连线，组成正确的对话并大声朗读 Match A with B to make up dialogues

| A | B |
|---|---|
| 她今天为什么没来上课？ | 因为他要出国留学，所以就辞职了。 |
| 他为什么要辞职？ | 因为感冒了，所以她没来上课。 |
| 他怎么回国了？ | 听说女朋友跟他分手了，所以不高兴。 |
| 你怎么又迟到了？ | 因为那儿的饭菜又好吃又便宜，所以我常去那儿。 |
| 这几天他怎么那么不高兴？ | 因为路上堵车，所以迟到了。 |
| 你怎么常去那儿吃饭？ | 他妈妈生病住院了，所以他回国了。 |

(提示：生词请查阅各类词典。)
(Tip: For new words, please refer to various dictionaries.)

(六) 和同学一起练习会话 Practice the conversation with your classmates

A：今天你去哪儿了？
B：我去超市买东西了。
A：你自己去的吗？
B：不，我和罗兰一起去的。

A：你买什么了？

B：我买了一个台灯、一盒巧克力、一个面包。

A：罗兰呢？

B：她买了两支毛笔、一瓶墨汁和一包宣纸。

（七）根据画线部分用疑问代词提问 Use interrogative pronouns to ask questions about the underlined parts

例：我常常去<u>超市</u>买东西。→ 你常常去哪儿买东西？

1. <u>超市里应有尽有，各种各样的东西又好又便宜</u>。→ _____

2. 我买了<u>一个台灯</u>。→ _____

3. 我想<u>跟罗兰一起</u>去。→ _____

4. 罗兰特喜欢<u>逛超市</u>。→ _____

5. 我<u>星期三</u>要上<u>书画课</u>。→ _____

6. 我买了<u>两支毛笔、一瓶墨汁和几张宣纸</u>。→ _____

7. 我<u>用微信</u>结账。→ _____

8. 手机提示（tíshì, to remind），<u>一共花了 118 元</u>。→ _____

（八）根据实际情况回答问题 Answer the questions according to the actual situations

1. 你喜欢逛超市吗？

2. 你们那儿的超市怎么样？

3. 你常去超市买东西吗？

4. 你会用微信支付吗？

5. 你见/用过毛笔、墨汁吗？

6. 你想不想学习书法或画画儿？

（九）和同学一起表演课文 Act out the text with your classmates

（十）读后说 Read the passage and say it

今天我和罗兰一起去超市买东西。我喜欢逛超市，超市里应有尽有，各种各样的东西又好又便宜，所以我常常去超市买东西。罗兰说，她也喜欢逛超市。

她问我都买了一些什么东西,我说,因为我的台灯坏了,所以,买了一个新台灯,还买了花生、果酱和巧克力。罗兰说,她星期三要上书画课,所以,买了两支毛笔、一些宣纸和一瓶墨汁。

(十一) 怎么表达 How to express

> dǎsuàn
> 打算  plan

A: Xīngqītiān nǐ dǎsuàn zuò shénme?
星期天 你打算 做 什么?
What will you do this Sunday?

B: Wǒ xiǎng qù yóu yǒng/huá bīng/huá xuě.
我 想 去游 泳/滑 冰/滑 雪。
I'd like to go swimming/skating/skiing.

(十二) 朗读中国经典诗词,请注意语音语调 Read aloud the classic Chinese poem and pay attention to the pronunciation and intonation

Yè Sù Shān Sì
**夜宿 山 寺**

[Táng] Lǐ Bái
[唐]李白(701—762)

Wēi lóu gāo bǎi chǐ, shǒu kě zhāi xīngchén.
危楼 高百尺,手可摘 星辰。

Bùgǎn gāo shēng yǔ, kǒng jīng tiānshang rén.
不敢 高 声 语,恐 惊 天上 人。

(十三) 请欣赏下列著名的词句 Please enjoy the following famous saying

Gōng dào zìrán chéng.
功 到自然 成。
If you try hard enough, you will succeed.

# 第二十九课 我买了一本英汉词典
## Lesson 29  I bought an English-Chinese dictionary

## 一 课文 Text

### （一）我们去书市看看吧

A：明天是星期六，我们去书市看看吧。

B：你想买什么书？

A：不一定要买，只是去看看。网上说，这个书市一年只有一次，规模很大。我想，我们学习汉语，就要多了解中国、了解中国社会、了解中国文化，就要多走走、多看看。

B：好吧，几点出发？

A：九点出发吧。

B：我们怎么去呢？

A：坐地铁去吧，不会堵车，一出站就到书市门口儿了。

B：要坐多长时间？

　　　　　　Chàbuduō xūyào yí gè xiǎoshí.
A：差不多需要一个小时。

　　　　　　Hǎo.
B：好。

　　　　　　Míngtiān wǒ bā diǎn wǔshí zài xuéxiào dōngmén děng nǐ,　bú jiàn bú sàn.
A：明天 我 八点 五十 在 学校　东门　等 你，不 见 不 散。

　　　　　　Bú jiàn bú sàn.
B：不 见 不 散。

---

Let's go to the book fair

A: Tomorrow is Saturday. Let's go to the book fair.

B: What book do you want to buy?

A: I don't have to buy any books. I'm just going to check it out. I've learned online that the book fair is held only once a year and is of a large scale. I think, when we learn Chinese, we need to know more about China, Chinese society and Chinese culture. We need to go out more and see more.

B: OK, what time shall we go?

A: Let's start off at nine.

B: How shall we go there?

A: Let's take the subway. We won't get stuck in traffic on the subway. As soon as we get out of the subway station, we'll be at the gate of the book fair.

B: How long does it take by subway?

A: It takes about an hour.

B: All right.

A: I'll meet you at the east gate of the school at 8:50 tomorrow. See you then.

B: See you then.

## （二）我买了一本英汉词典

　　　　　　Tīngshuō nǐmen qù shūshì le.
C：听说 你们 去 书市 了。

　　　　　　Shì.
B：是。

　　　　　　Dōu mǎi shénme shū le?
C：都 买 什么 书 了？

　　　　　　Wǒ mǎile yì běn Yīng-Hàn cídiǎn,　Màikè mǎile yì běn shìjiè dìtú cè.
B：我买了一本 英汉 词典，麦克买了一本 世界 地图 册。

　　　　　　Nàge shūshì gěi nǐ de gǎnjué zěnmeyàng?
C：那个 书市 给 你 的 感觉 怎么样？

B：我从来没见过那么大的书市，感觉规模很大，逛书市
的人很多，很热闹。

C：我也想抽空儿去看看。

B：去吧，值得一看，挺长见识的。

---

I bought an English-Chinese dictionary

C: I heard you went to the book fair.

B: Yes.

C: What books did you buy?

B: I bought an English-Chinese dictionary, and Mike bought a world atlas.

C: How do you feel about the book fair?

B: I've never seen such a big book fair before. It feels very big, crowded and busy.

C: I'd also like to go to check it out some time.

B: Go ahead. It's worth seeing and very informative.

## （三）我常在网上买东西

C：我想去书市看看。

D：你要买什么书？

C：我想买一本英汉词典。

D：你上网买吧。

C：网上买东西贵不贵？

D：一点儿都不贵，网购又方便又便宜，还能送货上门。我常常在网上买东西。

C：怎么在网上买书呢？

D：<ruby>非常<rt>Fēicháng</rt></ruby> <ruby>容易<rt>róngyi</rt></ruby>，<ruby>你<rt>nǐ</rt></ruby> <ruby>到<rt>dào</rt></ruby> <ruby>网上<rt>wǎngshang</rt></ruby> <ruby>商城<rt>shāngchéng</rt></ruby> <ruby>看看<rt>kànkan</rt></ruby> <ruby>就<rt>jiù</rt></ruby> <ruby>知道了<rt>zhīdào le</rt></ruby>。

C：我不怎么认识汉字，来这儿以后，还不会在 网上 买东西呢，我试试吧。
(Wǒ bù zěnme rènshi Hànzì, lái zhèr yǐhòu, hái bú huì zài wǎngshang mǎi dōngxi ne, wǒ shìshi ba.)

---

**I often buy stuff online**

C: I want to go to the book fair.

D: What book do you want to buy?

C: I want to buy an English-Chinese dictionary.

D: You can buy it online.

C: Is it expensive to buy things online?

D: It's not expensive at all. Online shopping is convenient and economical. And the goods can be delivered to your door. I often buy stuff online.

C: How do I buy books online?

D: Very easy. You can check out an online mall.

C: Because I don't know many Chinese characters, I haven't bought anything online yet since I came here. Let me try.

## 二  生词 New Words

| | | | | |
|---|---|---|---|---|
| 1 | 本 | běn | 量、名 | *a measure word for books*; book; notebook |
| 2 | 词典 | cídiǎn | 名 | dictionary |
| 3 | 书市 | shūshì | 名 | book fair; book market |
| 4 | 不一定 | bù yídìng | | not necessarily |
| | 一定 | yídìng | 形 | certain; definite |
| 5 | 只是 | zhǐshì | 副 | only |
| 6 | 规模 | guīmó | 名 | scale |
| 7 | 了解 | liǎojiě | 动 | to understand; to know |
| 8 | 社会 | shèhuì | 名 | society |

| | | | | |
|---|---|---|---|---|
| 9 | 文化 | wénhuà | 名 | culture |
| 10 | 地铁 | dìtiě | 名 | subway; metro |
| 11 | 堵车 | dǔ chē | 动 | traffic jam |
| 12 | 出站 | chū zhàn | | to get out of the station |
| 13 | 门口儿 | ménkǒur | 名 | gate; entrance |
| 14 | 差不多 | chàbuduō | 副、形 | almost; about |
| 15 | 不见不散 | bú jiàn bú sàn | | (let's) not leave without seeing each other (said when making an appointment) |
| | 见 | jiàn | 动 | to see; to meet with |
| | 散 | sàn | 动 | to disperse; to separate |
| 16 | 地图 | dìtú | 名 | map |
| 17 | 册 | cè | 名 | book; volume |
| 18 | 感觉 | gǎnjué | 动 | to feel |
| 19 | 从来 | cónglái | 副 | (*usu. used with a negative*) from the past till the present; always |
| 20 | 热闹 | rènao | 形 | lively; busy |
| 21 | 抽空儿 | chōu kòngr | 动 | to find time |
| 22 | 长 | zhǎng | 动 | to increase; to grow |
| 23 | 见识 | jiànshi | 名 | knowledge |
| 24 | 上网 | shàng wǎng | 动 | to surf the Internet |
| 25 | 网购 | wǎnggòu | 动 | to shop online |
| 26 | 送货上门 | sòng huò shàng mén | | to deliver goods to one's door |
| | 送 | sòng | 动 | to send; to deliver |
| 27 | 商城 | shāngchéng | 名 | shopping mall; store |
| 28 | 试 | shì | 动 | to try |

## 三　注释 Notes

### （一）不见不散

这是与别人约定时说的话，意思是：如果在约定的地点见不到对方的话，不要走开。例如：

This is what you say when you make an appointment with someone. It means that if you don't see each other at the appointed place, don't walk away. For example:

A：明天我八点五十在学校东门等你，不见不散。

B：不见不散。

### （二）一……都/也……。

汉语用"一……都/也……"强调完全否定。例如：

In Chinese, "一……都/也……" emphasizes total negation. For example:

1. A：你以前来过中国吗？

　　B：没有，一次也没来过。

2. 这种葡萄一点儿都不甜，酸的。

3. 我一本中文书也没看过。

4. 刚来时，我一句汉语都听不懂。

5. 这个电影我一点儿都不喜欢。

6. 这个菜一口都没吃。

### （三）我不怎么认识汉字，来这里以后，还不会在网上买东西呢。

疑问代词"怎么"在这里表示有一定程度，多用于否定式，语气比较委婉。例如：

The interrogative pronoun "怎么" here means "to a certain extent" and is often used in the negative, expressing a mild tone. For example:

不怎么认识 = 不大认识 / 不太认识

不怎么会说 = 不太会说

不怎么会写 = 不大会写

# 第二十九课 Lesson 29

不怎么好 = 不太好

我不怎么想去 = 我不太想去

## 四 练习 Exercises

（一）朗读下列发音相近的词语 Read aloud the following words and expressions with similar pronunciation

| shūshì | shǔshí | zhǐshì | zhīshi |
| 书市 | 属实 | 只是 | 知识 |
| chūfā | shūfǎ | shāngchéng | shàngchéng |
| 出发 | 书法 | 商城 | 上乘 |
| dìtú | dīdù | rènao | rěnǎo |
| 地图 | 低度 | 热闹 | 惹恼 |

（二）替换并朗读 Replace and read aloud

1. 明天是星期六，我们去 <u>书市</u> <u>看看</u>吧。

| 超市 | 买东西 |
| 展览馆 | 看展览 |
| 美术馆 | 看书画展 / 摄影展 |
| 滑雪场 | 滑雪 |
| 音乐厅 | 听音乐会 |
| 国际电影节 | 看电影 |

2. 我<u>买</u>了<u>一本英汉词典</u>。

| 买 | 一件羽绒服 |
| 看 | 一个书画展 |
| 借 | 一本中国地图册 |
| 拍 | 不少照片和视频 |
| 滑 | 两个小时雪 |
| 游 | 一个小时泳 |

3. 我常上网买东西。

购物
看电影
跟朋友聊天儿
跟爸爸妈妈视频
玩儿游戏
看新闻

4. 一点儿都不贵

不会　不饿　不累
不困　不想吃　不想去

5. 因为我还不怎么认识汉字，所以还不会在网上买东西。

不会看菜谱　　不会查词典
不能看中文报　不能读中文书
不会用中文写信　不会读这些诗

（提示：生词请查阅各类词典。）

(Tip: For new words, please refer to various dictionaries.)

（三）**选词填空并朗读下列句子** Choose the appropriate words to fill in the blanks and read aloud the following sentences

只是　就　了解　见　吧　差不多

1. A：明天是星期六，我们去书市看看_____。
   B：你想买什么书？
2. 不一定要买，_____看看。网上说，这个书市一年只有一次，规模很大。
3. 我想，我们学习汉语，就要多_____中国、了解中国社会、了解中国文化，就要多走走、多看看。

4. A：我们怎么去呢？

　　B：坐地铁去，不会堵车，出站＿＿＿＿到书市门口儿了。

5. A：坐地铁要多长时间？

　　B：＿＿＿＿要一个小时。

6. 明天我八点五十在学校东门等你，不＿＿＿＿不散。

　　本　了　认识　那么　都/也　挺

1. 听说你们去书市了，都买什么书＿＿＿＿？

2. 我买了一＿＿＿＿英汉词典，麦克买了一本世界地图册。

3. A：那个书市怎么样？

　　B：规模很大，我从来没有见过＿＿＿＿大的书市。逛书市的人很多，很热闹。

4. A：我也想抽空儿去看看。

　　B：去吧，值得一看，＿＿＿＿长见识的。

5. 你上网买吧。网上买一点儿＿＿＿＿不贵，网购又方便又便宜，还能送货上门。

6. 我不怎么＿＿＿＿汉字，来这里以后，还不会在网上买东西呢。

（四）用"差不多""不一定""有时候"等词语回答下列问题 Answer the following questions with "差不多", "不一定" or "有时候"

1. A：你现在能认多少汉字？

　　B：＿＿＿＿＿＿＿＿＿＿＿＿＿＿＿＿＿＿＿。

2. A：你晚上能睡多长时间？

　　B：＿＿＿＿＿＿＿＿＿＿＿＿＿＿＿＿＿＿＿。

3. A：从你们国家到中国有多远？

　　B：＿＿＿＿＿＿＿＿＿＿＿＿＿＿＿＿＿＿＿。

4. A：从你住的地方走到教室要多长时间？

　　B：＿＿＿＿＿＿＿＿＿＿＿＿＿＿＿＿＿＿＿。

5. A：你每天大约学习几个小时？

   B：_____。

6. A：你每天预习生词和课文需要多长时间？做作业呢？

   B：_____。

（五）和同学一起练习下列会话 Practice the following conversations with your classmates

1. A：别怕，一学就会。

   B：我试试吧。

2. A：这东西好吃吗？

   B：你尝尝看，我觉得味道不错。

3. A：这个歌儿好听吗？

   B：你听听就知道了。

4. A：这个游戏好玩儿不好玩儿？

   B：你玩玩儿看，挺好玩儿的。

5. A：这茶好喝吗？

   B：我尝了尝，不太好喝。

6. A：这本书好看吗？

   B：你看看就知道了，我觉得非常有意思。

（六）你是 A，请你向 B 提问 Supposing you are A, ask B questions

A：_____？

B：我喜欢逛书店，不喜欢逛商店。

A：_____？

B：我朋友和我不一样，她喜欢逛商店，不喜欢逛书店。

A：_____？

B：我觉得现在逛书店的人越来越少了。

A：_____？

B：因为很多人都在网上买书。

A: _____?

B：我常常网购，网购又方便又便宜，还能送货上门。

（七）根据实际情况回答问题 Answer the questions according to the actual situations

1. 周末你常去什么地方？
2. 上个周末你去哪儿了？
3. 你是什么时间去的？
4. 你是和谁一起去的？
5. 你（们）是怎么去的？
6. 都买（看）了什么东西？

（八）和同学一起表演课文 Act out the text with your classmates

（九）自由表达 Free expression

看世界地图，说出你的国家在什么位置，并且填写以下表格，然后向大家报告。

Look at the map of the world and describe the location of your country. Fill in the form below and report it to everyone.

| | |
|---|---|
| guómíng<br>国名 country name | |
| wèizhì<br>位置 location | |
| qìhòu<br>气候 climate | |
| miànjī<br>面积 area | |
| shǒudū<br>首都 capital | |
| guóqí<br>国旗 national flag | |
| guógē<br>国歌 national anthem | |

| | |
|---|---|
| rénkǒu<br>人口 population | |
| yǔyán<br>语言 language | |
| mínzú<br>民族 ethnic group | |
| tèchǎn<br>特产 specialty | |
| Guóqìng Jié<br>国庆节 National Day | |
| huòbì<br>货币 currency | |

（十）读后说 Read the passage and say it

昨天我和麦克一起去书市了，我们是上午九点从学校出发的。我们是坐地铁去的，坐地铁很方便，也很便宜，还不怕堵车。下了地铁一出站就到书市门口儿了。这个书市在一个大公园里，来书市看书、买书的人特别多，非常热闹。我从来没有见过那么大的书市，真长见识。我们逛了差不多两个小时，我买了一本英汉词典，麦克买了一本世界地图册，然后就高高兴兴地回来了。

（十一）怎么表达 How to express

> lèguān
> 乐观　optimism

Wǒ hěn lèguān.
1. 我 很 乐观。
   I am very optimistic.

Wǒ shì gè lèguānzhǔyìzhě / lètiānpài.
2. 我 是 个 乐观主义者 / 乐天派。
   I'm an optimist.

Wǒ duì qiántú fēicháng lèguān.
3. 我 对 前途 非常 乐观。
   I'm full of optimism for the future.

## 第二十九课 Lesson 29

**（十二）朗读中国经典诗词，请注意语音语调** Read aloud the classic Chinese poem and pay attention to the pronunciation and intonation

Tiānjìngshā　Qiū Sī
**天净沙·秋思**

[Yuán] Mǎ Zhìyuǎn　　　　yuē　　　　　　hòu
〔元〕马　致远（约1251—1321后）

Kū téng lǎo shù hūn yā,
枯藤老树昏鸦，

xiǎo qiáo liúshuǐ rénjiā,
小桥流水人家，

gǔ dào xīfēng shòu mǎ.
古道西风瘦马。

Xīyáng xī xià,
夕阳西下，

duànchángrén zài tiānyá.
断肠人在天涯。

**（十三）请欣赏下列著名的词句** Please enjoy the following famous saying

Dú shū pò wàn juàn,　xià bǐ rú yǒu shén.
读书破万卷，下笔如有神。

After you have read more than ten thousand volumes,

you will find it easy to write as if God were there helping you.

# 第三十课 Lesson 30
## Dì-sānshí kè
## Wǒ láile sān gè duō yuè le
## 我来了三个多月了
### I've been here for more than three months

## 一 课文 Text

（A 在跟她的一个在中国留学的朋友视频聊天儿……）

A：Zěnmeyàng a, nǐ de xuéxiào?
怎么样啊，你的学校？

B：Wǒmen dàxué hěn hǎo.
我们大学很好。

A：Nǐ yǐjīng qùle kuài bànnián le ba?
你已经去了快半年了吧？

B：Méiyǒu. Wǒ láile sān gè duō yuè le.
没有。我来了三个多月了。

A：Shēnghuó shang shì bu shì dōu xíguàn le?
生活上是不是都习惯了？

B：Chàbuduō dōu xíguàn le. Duìle, wǒ gěi nǐ fā de zhàopiàn nǐ shōudàole méiyǒu?
差不多都习惯了。对了，我给你发的照片你收到了没有？

A：Nǐ fā de zhàopiàn, wǒ dōu shōudào le. Měi yì zhāng zhàopiàn wǒ búdàn dōu kàn le, érqiě kànde hěn zǐxì. Nǐmen de xiàoyuán zhēn piàoliang, dàochù dōu shì lǜ shù hé xiānhuā, hǎoxiàng huāyuán yíyàng.
你发的照片，我都收到了。每一张照片我不但都看了，而且看得很仔细。你们的校园真漂亮，到处都是绿树和鲜花，好像花园一样。

B：Shìde. Hái yǒu yí gè hú, wǒ zuì xǐhuan nàge hú le. Wǒ ài zài hú biānr
是的。还有一个湖，我最喜欢那个湖了。我爱在湖边儿

第三十课 Lesson 30

散步，也常和同学们在湖边儿草地上看书、聊天儿。

A：我看湖中间有一座小桥，湖边儿还立着一面墙，那是什么墙？

B：啊，那叫万国墙，上面刻着世界上一百多个国家的名字。

A：这就是说，你们大学有从世界上一百多个国家去的留学生？

B：对。同学们来自世界各国，虽然有很多不同，不同的肤色、不同的语言、不同的文化、不同的生活习惯，但是大家的目的是相同的，都是为了学习汉语、了解中国、了解中国文化才来到这里，来追求自己的人生梦想。

A：这就是一个小"联合国"啊！

B：是，大家都这么说。

A：你们大学有多少留学生？

B：我不太清楚，听说有上万人呢。

A：真好！我看你们学校充满活力。

· 119 ·

    Shì. Zhè shì yí gè dú shū de hǎo dìfang, wǒ xǐhuan wǒmen de xuéxiào.
B：是。这是一个读书的好 地方，我喜欢 我们 的学校。

    Wǒ zhēn xiànmù nǐ! Néng shàng zhème hǎo de dàxué.
A：我 真 羡慕你！能 上 这么好 的大学。

    Nǐ yě kuài diǎnr dào zhèr lái ba.
B：你 也 快 点儿 到 这儿 来吧。

    Děngzhe wǒ ba.
A：等着 我吧。

---

**I've been here for more than three months**

(A is video chatting with a friend who is studying in China.)

A: How is your university?

B: Our university is very good.

A: You've been there for almost half a year, right?

B: No, I've been here for over three months.

A: Are you used to the life there?

B: I'm almost used to living here. By the way, have you received the photos I sent you?

A: I've received all the photos you sent me. I not only looked at every single picture, but also looked at them carefully. Your campus is so beautiful. There are green trees and flowers everywhere. It looks like a garden.

B: Yes. There is also a lake. I like the lake best. I love walking by the lake, and I often read and chat with my classmates on the grass by the lake.

A: I see a small bridge in the middle of the lake. There is a wall beside the lake. What is that wall?

B: Ah, it's called the 10,000-country wall. On the wall are carved the names of more than one hundred countries in the world.

A: That is to say, your university has international students from more than one hundred countries?

B: Yes. Students from all over the world, despite different skin colors, languages, cultures, and habits, have the same goal, that is, to learn Chinese and to understand China and Chinese culture. We all came here to pursue our dreams of life.

A: It's a little United Nations.

B: Yeah, a lot of people say that.

A: How many international students are there in your university?

B: I'm not sure. I heard there were ten thousand.

A: It's nice! I think your university is full of vitality.

B: Yes. It's a good place to study. I like our university.

A: How I envy you! Going to such a great university!

B: Come here as soon as you can.

A: Wait for me.

## 二 生词 New Words

| | | | | |
|---|---|---|---|---|
| 1 | 生活 | shēnghuó | 名 | living; life |
| 2 | 习惯 | xíguàn | 动、名 | to get used to; habit |
| 3 | 收到 | shōudào | 动 | to receive; to obtain |
| | 收 | shōu | 动 | to receive; to collect |
| 4 | 不但 | búdàn | 连 | not only |
| 5 | 而且 | érqiě | 连 | but also |
| 6 | 仔细 | zǐxì | 形 | careful |
| 7 | 校园 | xiàoyuán | 名 | campus |
| 8 | 到处 | dàochù | 副 | everywhere |
| 9 | 绿 | lǜ | 形 | green |
| 10 | 树 | shù | 名 | tree |
| 11 | 鲜花 | xiānhuā | 名 | (fresh) flower |
| 12 | 好像 | hǎoxiàng | 动 | to seem; as if |
| 13 | 花园 | huāyuán | 名 | garden |
| 14 | 湖 | hú | 名 | lake |
| 15 | 散步 | sàn bù | 动 | to take a walk |
| 16 | 草地 | cǎodì | 名 | lawn; ground covered with grass |
| 17 | 座 | zuò | 名、量 | *a measure word for mountains, buildings, and other similar immovable objects* |
| 18 | 桥 | qiáo | 名 | bridge |
| 19 | 立 | lì | 动 | to set up; to stand |
| 20 | 面 | miàn | 量 | *a measure word for flat things, such as walls, flags, mirrors, etc.* |

| | | | | |
|---|---|---|---|---|
| 21 | 墙 | qiáng | 名 | wall |
| 22 | 上面 | shàngmiàn | 名 | surface of sth. |
| 23 | 刻 | kè | 动 | to sculpture; to engrave; to carve |
| 24 | 虽然 | suīrán | 连 | though; although |
| 25 | 不同 | bù tóng | | different |
| 26 | 肤色 | fūsè | 名 | skin color |
| 27 | 但是 | dànshì | 连 | but; yet |
| 28 | 目的 | mùdì | 名 | purpose; aim |
| 29 | 相同 | xiāngtóng | 形 | same |
| 30 | 为了 | wèile | 介 | for; in order to |
| 31 | 梦想 | mèngxiǎng | 动、名 | dream |
| 32 | 人们 | rénmen | 名 | people |
| 33 | 清楚 | qīngchu | 动、形 | clear |
| 34 | 充满 | chōngmǎn | 动 | to be full of |
| 35 | 活力 | huólì | 名 | vigor |
| 36 | 地方 | dìfang | 名 | place |
| 37 | 羡慕 | xiànmù | 动 | to admire; to envy |
| 38 | 上 | shàng | 动 | to go to (school, work, etc.) |

**专名** Zhuānmíng  Proper Noun

联合国  Liánhéguó  the United Nations

## 三 注释 Notes

（一）主语 + 动词 +（了）+ 时间量词 Subject + verb +（了）+ complement of duration

时量补语表示动作或状态持续的时间。

基本格式是：主语 + 动词 +（了）+ 时间量词

  如：我   +   来   +   了   +   三个多月了。

Complement of duration is used to express the duration of an action or a state.

The basic pattern is: Subject + verb +（了）+ complement of duration

例如：For example:

     Nǐ xuéle duō cháng shíjiān de Hànyǔ le?
1. A：你 学了 多 长 时间 的 汉语 了？

     Wǒ yǐjīng xuéle bànnián le.
  B：我 已经 学了 半年 了。

    Wǒmen yì xīngqī shàng wǔ tiān kè.
2. 我们 一星期 上 五天课。

    Zuótiān wǎnshang wǒ shuìle bā gè xiǎoshí.
3. 昨天 晚上 我 睡了八个小时。

    Wǒ yǐjīng zuòle liǎng gè xiǎoshí zuòyè le, dànshì hái méiyǒu zuòwán.
4. 我 已经 做了 两 个 小时 作业 了，但是 还 没有 做完。

注意 Note：1. 我学了半年了。（说话时还在学 One is still learning when he/she speaks.）

     2. 我学了半年。（说话时可以在学，也可以不学了 One may be learning or not when he/she speaks.）

（二）对了，我给你发的照片，你收到没有？

"对了"是插入语，表示谈话中突然想起了某件事儿。例如：

"对了" is a parenthesis. It means something suddenly comes to one's mind during a conversation. For example:

  1. 对了，你刚才和我说了什么？

  2. 对了，我忘跟你说了。

（三）不但

连词"不但"用在递进复句的前半句里，下半句里通常用连词"而且、并且"或副词"也、还"等相呼应。

The conjunction "不但" is used in the first half of a progressive complex sentence, usually echoed by the conjunction "而且 / 并且" or the adverb "也 / 还", etc. in the second half of the sentence. For example:

1. 这种苹果不但好看，而且好吃。
2. 学校食堂的饭菜不但品种多，还便宜。

## 四 练习 Exercises

（一）朗读 Read aloud

1. 朗读下列发音相近的词语 Read aloud the following words and expressions with similar pronunciation

| piàoliang | piāoyáng | hǎoxiàng | hǎo xiāng |
| 漂亮 | 飘扬 | 好像 | 好香 |
| dàochù | dàolù | lǜ shù | lìshū |
| 到处 | 道路 | 绿树 | 隶书 |
| xiānhuā | xiánhuà | sàn bù | sān bù |
| 鲜花 | 闲话 | 散步 | 三步 |

2. 朗读下列词组 Read aloud the phrases

| děngzhe | kànzhe | shuōzhe | tīngzhe |
| 等着 | 看着 | 说着 | 听着 |
| zuòzhe | zǒuzhe | kūzhe | xiàozhe |
| 坐着 | 走着 | 哭着 | 笑着 |
| fā zhàopiàn | fā shìpín | fā xìnxī | fā wēixìn |
| 发照片 | 发视频 | 发信息 | 发微信 |

xiàoyuán hěn piàoliang
校园 很 漂亮

fēngjǐng hěn piàoliang
风景 很 漂亮

huàr huàde hěn piàoliang
画儿画得 很 漂亮

zì xiěde hěn piàoliang
字写得很 漂亮

## 第三十课 Lesson 30

（二）替换并朗读 Replace and read aloud

1. 你已经<u>去</u>了快<u>半年</u>了吧？

| | |
|---|---|
| 学 | 一年 |
| 干 | 一个星期 |
| 做 | 一个小时 |
| 画 | 一天 |
| 写 | 四十分钟 |

2. 上面<u>刻</u>着世界上一百多个国家的<u>名字</u>呢。

| | |
|---|---|
| 挂 | 我们国家的国旗 |
| 写 | 我的名字 |
| 画 | 一幅画儿 |
| 站 | 很多同学 |
| 坐 | 各国的代表 |

3. 到处都是<u>绿树</u>。

| | | |
|---|---|---|
| 鲜花 | 人 | 水 |
| 汽车 | 水果 | 书 |

4. 我喜欢在<u>湖边</u>散步。

| | | |
|---|---|---|
| 海边 | 河边 | 校园里 |
| 操场上 | 公园里 | 树林里 |

5. 我真羡慕你！<u>能上这么好的大学</u>。

读了那么多的书
能画那么好的画儿
钢琴弹得那么好
汉字写得那么漂亮
汉语说得那么流利
足球踢得那么棒

（提示：生词请查阅各类词典。）

(Tip: For new words, please refer to various dictionaries.)

（三）选词填空并朗读下列句子 Choose the appropriate words to fill in the appropriate blanks and read aloud the following sentences

> 一样　从　而且　了　目的　在　着　为了

1. A：你已经去中国快半年了吧？
   B：我来了三个多月_____。
2. 你发的照片，我不但都看了，_____看得很仔细。
3. 你们的校园真漂亮，到处都是绿树和鲜花，好像花园_____。
4. 学校里还有一个湖，我最喜欢那个湖了。我爱_____湖边儿散步，也常和同学们在湖边儿草地上看书、聊天儿。
5. A：我看湖中间有一座小桥，湖边还立_____一面墙，那是什么墙？
   B：那叫万国墙，上面刻着一百多个国家的名字。
6. 就是说，你们大学有_____世界上一百多个国家去的留学生。
7. 同学们来自世界各国，有很多不同，不同的肤色、不同的语言、不同的文化、不同的生活习惯，但是大家的_____是相同的。
8. 大家都是_____学习汉语、了解中国、了解中国文化来到这里，来追求自己的人生梦想。

（四）将A、B两列连线，组成正确的句子，然后朗读 Match A with B to make sentences and then read the sentences aloud

1.
| A | B |
| --- | --- |
| 我来这儿不但学了汉语， | 而且还有很多中国学生。 |
| 她不但聪明， | 而且汉字也写得很漂亮。 |
| 我们大学不但有外国留学生， | 而且还交了不少朋友。 |
| 他不但汉语说得好， | 而且还关心我们的生活。 |
| 老师不但关心我们的学习， | 而且大人也很喜欢看。 |
| 这个电影不但孩子喜欢看， | 而且漂亮，我很喜欢她。 |

2.　　　　A　　　　　　　　　　　　　　B

我们大学虽然离市区很远，　　　　但是屋子里很暖和。
中国北方的冬天虽然很冷，　　　　但是非常快乐。
虽然我每天都很忙，　　　　　　　但是因为常常不上课，所以学
　　　　　　　　　　　　　　　　得不太好。

这篇文章虽然比较长，　　　　　　可是进步很快。
同学们虽然来自不同的国家，　　　但是生词不多，我读懂了。
虽然他学得时间不长，　　　　　　但是交通很方便。
虽然汉语对我来说比较难，　　　　但是大家都友好相处，像兄弟
　　　　　　　　　　　　　　　　姐妹一样。

虽然他很聪明，　　　　　　　　　但是我越学越觉得有意思。

3.　　　　A　　　　　　　　　　　　　　B

这面墙上　　　　　　　　　　　　坐着听课。
教室里　　　　　　　　　　　　　戴着耳机在听音乐呢。
她们在湖边　　　　　　　　　　　站着讲课。
老师在上面　　　　　　　　　　　刻着一百多个国家的名字。
我们在下面　　　　　　　　　　　坐着聊天儿呢
他　　　　　　　　　　　　　　　挂着一张世界地图

（提示：生词请查阅各类词典。）

(Tip: For new words, please refer to various dictionaries.)

（五）完成下列句子并大声朗读 Complete the following sentences and read them aloud

例：<u>你们的学校</u>充满活力。

| 我们的未来 | 我对学好汉语 | 她的眼里 |
| 我的留学生活 | 生日晚会上 | 同学们身上 |

1. _____ 充满快乐。
2. _____ 充满朝气和力量。
3. _____ 充满泪水。
4. _____ 充满希望。

5. _____ 充满信心。

6. _____ 充满歌声和笑声。

## 小词典

| 歌声 | gēshēng | 名 | sound of singing |
| 笑声 | xiàoshēng | 名 | laughter |
| 希望 | xīwàng | 名 | hope |
| 泪水 | lèishuǐ | 名 | tear; teardrop |
| 信心 | xìnxīn | 名 | confidence |
| 朝气 | zhāoqì | 名 | youthful spirit |
| 力量 | lìliàng | 名 | strength |

（六）根据实际情况回答问题 Answer the questions according to the actual situations

1. 你来中国多长时间了？
2. 你们大学的校园怎么样？
3. 你们大学有多少留学生？
4. 你觉得你们班上的同学有什么不同？
5. 你现在习惯在中国的生活了吗？
6. 请说说你的留学生活。

（七）和同学一起练习下面的会话 Practice the following conversation with your classmates

（在游泳馆 At the natatorium）

A：你游了多长时间了？

B：我游了一个钟头（zhōngtóu, hour）了。

A：游了多远？

B：我游一会儿休息一会儿，游了差不多两千米吧。你呢？

A：我刚来，才游了五百米。

（过了一会儿 After a while）

B：怎么样？上去吧。

A：你不游了？你先上去吧，我再游一会儿。

B：好的。

（八）和同学一起表演课文 Act out the text with your classmates

（九）读后说 Read the passage and say it

今天跟朋友视频聊天儿，她问我，我们学校怎么样，我说我们的校园很美，到处是绿地和鲜花，还有一个湖，湖中有一座小桥，湖边儿还立着一面万国墙，上面刻着一百多个国家的名字。我常常在湖边儿散步，也常和同学在湖边儿草地上读书和聊天儿。

我们大学有上万名来自世界各国的留学生。虽然我们有很多不同，不同的肤色、不同的语言、不同的文化、不同的生活习惯，但是大家有一个共同的目的，都是为了学习汉语、了解中国、了解中国文化，所以，人们说我们大学是个小"联合国"。

朋友说，我们的大学充满了活力，非常羡慕我。我说，这是一个读书的好地方，我很喜欢我们的学校，也希望她能快点儿来。

（十）怎么表达 How to express

| xiànmù |
| 羡慕   envy; admiration |

1. Wǒ zhēn xiànmù nǐ, néng chū guó liú xué.
   我 真 羡慕 你，能 出 国 留 学。
   I really envy you being able to study abroad.

2. Tā néng qù Běijīng shàng dàxué, zhēn xìngyùn!
   他 能 去 北京 上 大学，真 幸运！
   He is lucky to go to university in Beijing.

3. Wǒ tài xiànmù nǐ le, yǒu zhème yí gè hǎo zhàngfu / qīzǐ.
   我 太 羡慕 你 了，有 这么 一个 好 丈夫 / 妻子。
   I envy you so much for having such a good husband/wife.

**(十一) 朗读中国经典诗词，请注意语音语调** Read aloud the classic Chinese poem and pay attention to the pronunciation and intonation

### Fēng Qiáo Yè Bó
### 枫 桥 夜 泊

[Táng] Zhāng Jì　　yuē
[唐] 张 继（？—约779）

Yuè luò wū tí shuāng mǎn tiān, jiāng fēng yúhuǒ duì chóu mián.
月落乌啼霜满天，江枫渔火对愁眠。

Gūsū chéng wài Hánshān Sì, yèbàn zhōngshēng dào kè chuán.
姑苏城外寒山寺，夜半钟声到客船。

**(十二) 请欣赏下列著名的词句** Please enjoy the following famous saying

Jiān ài fēi gōng, shàng xián shàng néng.
兼爱非攻，尚贤尚能。

Love universally and do not attack each other;

Look up to and admire virtuous and talented people.

# 第三十一课 Lesson 31
## 我请小时工帮我收拾房间
### Wǒ qǐng xiǎoshígōng bāng wǒ shōushi fángjiān
### I hired an hourly worker to help me clean my room

## 一 课文 Text

（马丁请朋友吉米来自己的房间）

马丁：请进。
Mǎdīng: Qǐng jìn.

吉米：啊，你的房间怎么变得这么干净整齐呀？墙上还挂着两幅山水画，窗台上摆着一盆花儿，整个屋子布置得这么漂亮。
Jímǐ: À, nǐ de fángjiān zěnme biànde zhème gānjìng zhěngqí ya? Qiáng shang hái guàzhe liǎng fú shānshuǐhuà, chuāngtái shang bǎizhe yì pén huār, zhěnggè wūzi bùzhì de zhème piàoliang.

马丁：漂亮吧？
Mǎdīng: Piàoliang ba?

吉米：怎么回事儿呀？我上次来，你这屋里像什么，你还记得吗？
Jímǐ: Zěnme huí shìr ya? Wǒ shàng cì lái, nǐ zhè wū li xiàng shénme, nǐ hái jìde ma?

马丁：像什么？
Mǎdīng: Xiàng shénme?

吉米：像狗屋一样，乱得简直没法儿进。
Jímǐ: Xiàng gǒuwū yíyàng, luàn de jiǎnzhí méifǎr jìn.

马丁：你真会开玩笑。我叫马丁，我的屋子只能是"马屋"
Mǎdīng: Nǐ zhēn huì kāi wánxiào. Wǒ jiào Mǎdīng, wǒ de wūzi zhǐ néng shì "mǎwū"

· 131 ·

a.
啊。

吉米： Hāhā, nà zěnme yíxiàzi biànchéng zhèyàng le?
吉米： 哈哈，那怎么一下子变成这样了？

Mǎdīng: Yīnwèi wǒ qǐngle yí ge xiǎoshígōng, shì tā bāng wǒ shōushi de.
马丁： 因为我请了一个小时工，是她帮我收拾的。

Jímǐ: Xiǎoshígōng? Shénme xiǎoshígōng?
吉米： 小时工？什么小时工？

Mǎdīng: Jiù shì ànzhào xiǎoshí fùfèi de gōngrén a.
马丁： 就是按照小时付费的工人啊。

Jímǐ: Nǐ shì cóng nǎr qǐng de?
吉米： 你是从哪儿请的？

Mǎdīng: Wǒ shì cóng jiāzhèng fúwù gōngsī qǐng de, wǒ gěi tāmen dǎle ge diànhuà, tāmen jiù pài tā lái le.
马丁： 我是从家政服务公司请的，我给他们打了个电话，他们就派她来了。

Jímǐ: Nǐ shì zěnme zhīdào zhège xìnxī de?
吉米： 你是怎么知道这个信息的？

Mǎdīng: Shì Lín lǎoshī gàosu wǒ de. Shàng xīngqī wǒ gǎnmào le, bìng de hěn lìhai, Lín lǎoshī lái kàn wǒ, tā kàn wǒ wūzi luànqībāzāo de, jiù jiànyì wǒ zuìhǎo qǐng ge xiǎoshígōng.
马丁： 是林老师告诉我的。上星期我感冒了，病得很厉害，林老师来看我，她看我屋子乱七八糟的，就建议我最好请个小时工。

Jímǐ: Xiǎoshígōng yì zhōu lái jǐ cì?
吉米： 小时工一周来几次？

Mǎdīng: Yì xīngqī jiù lái yí cì, zài wǒ zhèr gàn yí ge xiǎoshí, zài dào gébì gàn yí ge xiǎoshí.
马丁： 一星期就来一次，在我这儿干一个小时，再到隔壁干一个小时。

Jímǐ: Wǒ yě qǐng tā bāng wǒ shōushi fángjiān, kěyǐ ma?
吉米： 我也请她帮我收拾房间，可以吗？

Mǎdīng: Wǒ xiǎng méi wèntí.
马丁： 我想没问题。

# Lesson 31  第三十一课

---

**I hired an hourly worker to help me clean my room**

(Martin invited his friend Jimmy to his room...)

Martin: Please come in.

Jimmy: Oh, how come your room is so clean and tidy? Look at the two landscape paintings hanging on the wall and the flowerpot on the windowsill. The whole room is so beautifully furnished.

Martin: It's pretty, isn't it?

Jimmy: What's going on here? The last time I was here, what was your room like? Do you remember?

Martin: Like what?

Jimmy: It was like a doghouse. It was too messy to get into.

Martin: You must be joking! My name is Martin, and my house must be a horse stable. (Note: "Horse" is called "马 (mǎ)" in Chinese.)

Jimmy: Ha! Ha! How did it change to this all of a sudden?

Martin: I hired an hourly worker who cleaned it up for me.

Jimmy: Hourly worker? What is an hourly worker?

Martin: A worker who is paid by the hour.

Jimmy: Where did you hire your hourly worker?

Martin: I hired her from a housekeeping company. I called their office, and they sent her.

Jimmy: How did you get this information?

Martin: Ms. Lin told me about it. I caught a cold last week and was very ill. Ms. Lin came to see me. She looked around my messy room and suggested that I hire an hourly worker.

Jimmy: How many times a week does the hourly worker come?

Martin: She comes once a week, working an hour for me and another hour next door.

Jimmy: Can I also ask her to help me clean the room?

Martin: No problem, I think.

## 二 生词 New Words

| | | | | |
|---|---|---|---|---|
| 1 | 小时工 | xiǎoshígōng | 名 | hourly worker |
|   | 小时   | xiǎoshí     | 名 | hour |
| 2 | 收拾   | shōushi     | 动 | to clear up; to put in order |
| 3 | 变     | biàn        | 动 | to change |
| 4 | 干净   | gānjìng     | 形 | clean |
| 5 | 整齐   | zhěngqí     | 形 | in good order; tidy |
| 6 | 挂     | guà         | 动 | to hang |

| 7 | 幅 | fú | 量 | *a measure word for paintings* |
| 8 | 山水画 | shānshuǐhuà | 名 | landscape painting |
| 9 | 窗台 | chuāngtái | 名 | windowsill |
| 10 | 摆 | bǎi | 动 | to place; to put |
| 11 | 盆 | pén | 名 | pot |
| 12 | 整个 | zhěnggè | 形 | whole |
| 13 | 屋子 | wūzi | 名 | room |
| 14 | 布置 | bùzhì | 动 | to fix up; to arrange |
| 15 | 回 | huí | 量 | (*indicating frequency of occurrence*) time |
| 16 | 上次 | shàng cì | | last time |
| 17 | 记得 | jìde | 动 | to remember |
| 18 | 狗屋 | gǒuwū | 名 | doghouse |
| 19 | 乱 | luàn | 形 | in a mess |
| 20 | 开玩笑 | kāi wánxiào | | to crack a joke; to make fun of |
| 21 | 一下子 | yíxiàzi | 副 | in a short while; suddenly |
| 22 | 成 | chéng | 动 | to become |
| 23 | 按照 | ànzhào | 介 | according to |
| 24 | 付费 | fùfèi | 动 | to pay |
| 25 | 工人 | gōngrén | 名 | worker |
| 26 | 家政 | jiāzhèng | 名 | housekeeping; homemaking |
| 27 | 服务 | fúwù | 动 | to serve |
| 28 | 信息 | xìnxī | 名 | information |
| 29 | 感冒 | gǎnmào | 动 | to have a cold; to catch a cold |
| 30 | 病 | bìng | 动、名 | to fall ill; illness |
| 31 | 厉害 | lìhai | 形 | serious; intense; terrible |

| 32 | 乱七八糟 | luànqībāzāo | | in a mess |
| 33 | 建议 | jiànyì | 动、名 | to suggest; suggestion |
| 34 | 最好 | zuìhǎo | 副 | had better |
| | 最 | zuì | 副 | most |
| 35 | 就 | jiù | 副 | only; merely; just |
| 36 | 隔壁 | gébì | 名 | next door |

## 三 注释 Notes

（一）他们就派她来了。

汉语表达"让某人做某事"的意思时，用兼语句。这类句子的语序是：
主语 + 使令动词（请、叫、让、派）+ 兼语（宾语/主语）+ 动词 + 宾语

When expressing the meaning of "let someone do something" in Chinese, we use the pivotal sentence. The order of this kind of sentence is:

Subject + imperative verb ( 请 ask, 叫 call, 让 let, 派 send) + pivot (object/subject) + verb + object

1. 公司派她来的。
2. 我也想请她帮我收拾房间。
3. 老师建议我请个小时工。

（二）你是怎么知道这个信息的？

汉语用"是……的"强调已经发生或完成的动作的时间、地点、方式、目的、施事和受事等。

In Chinese, "是……的" is used to emphasize the time, place, way, purpose, agent, and patient, etc. of an action that has happened or completed.

1. 这个信息是林老师告诉我的。
2. 我是跟朋友一起来的。
3. 麦克是从美国来的。

（三）一星期就来一次。

"次"是动量词，表示动作的次数。

"次" is a measure word for frequency, indicating how many times an action happens.

汉语的动量词有：次、回、下等。

Chinese measure words of frequency include: 次, 回, 下, etc.

汉语的时量词有：分钟、天、星期、月、年等。

Chinese measure words of duration include: 分钟, 天, 星期, 月, 年, etc.

## 四 练习 Exercises

（一）朗读下列发音相近的词语 Read aloud the following words and expressions with similar pronunciation

| zěnme | zhème | gānjìng | gànjǐng |
| 怎么 | 这么 | 干净 | 干警 |
| zhěngqí | zhèngqì | bùzhì | bùzhǐ |
| 整齐 | 正气 | 布置 | 不只 |
| shōushi | shǒushì | xìnxī | xīnxì |
| 收拾 | 首饰 | 信息 | 心细 |

（二）替换并朗读 Replace and read aloud

1. 布置得这么漂亮

| 收拾 | 整齐 |
| 学 | 好 |
| 搞 | 乱 |
| 画 | 好看 |
| 照 | 美 |

2. 我病得很厉害。

| 烧 | 咳嗽 | 头疼 |
| 嗓子疼 | 肚子疼 | 拉肚子拉 |

3. 是<u>小时工帮我收拾</u>的。

> 老师教我　　公司派她来
> 朋友送给我　同学给我照
> 丹尼斯画

4. <u>整个</u>屋子怎么这么<u>干净整齐</u>？

> 你的房间　　　大
> 你们的校园　　漂亮
> 他汉语说得　　好
> 快递费　　　　便宜
> 这个手机　　　好用

5. <u>墙上还挂着两幅</u>山水画。

> 窗台上还摆　　一盆花儿
> 她头上还戴　　一顶红帽子
> 他背上背　　　一个旅行包
> 他手里拿　　　一张旅游图
> 她身上穿　　　一件羽绒服

6. 每星期<u>来</u>一次，一次一个小时。

> 收拾　　按摩　教
> 辅导我　学　　游

（**提示**：生词请查阅各类词典。）

(Tip: For new words, please refer to various dictionaries.)

（三）**选词填空并朗读下列句子** Choose the appropriate words to fill in the blanks and read aloud the following sentences

> 建议　会　像　着　请　给

1. 啊，你的房间怎么变得这么干净整齐啊？墙上还挂_____两幅画儿，窗台上摆_____一盆花，整个屋子布置得这么漂亮。

2. 这是怎么回事儿啊？我上次来，你这屋里_____什么，你还记得吗？

3. A：屋子像狗屋一样，乱得简直没法儿进。
   B：你真_____开玩笑。我叫马丁，我的屋子只能是"马屋"啊。

4. A：怎么一下子变成这样了？
   B：因为我_____了一个小时工，是她帮我收拾的。

5. A：你是从哪儿请的？
   B：我是从家政服务公司请的，我_____他们打了个电话，他们就派她来了。

6. A：你是怎么知道这个信息的？
   B：是林老师告诉我的。上星期我感冒了，病得很厉害，林老师来看我，她看我屋子里乱七八糟的，就_____我最好请个小时工。

（四）你是 A，请你就画线部分向 B 提问 Supposing you are A, ask B questions about the underlined parts

1. A：_____？
   B：我也请她<u>帮我收拾房间</u>。

2. A：_____？
   B：我们让<u>老师</u>说慢点儿。

3. A：_____？
   B：老师叫<u>我</u>回答问题。

4. A：_____？
   B：是<u>公司</u>派我来中国留学的。

5. A：_____？
   B：我想请她<u>帮我们拍照</u>。

6. A：_____？
   B：我请他<u>给我修修自行车</u>（zìxíngchē, bicycle）。

（五）将 A、B 两列连线，组成正确的对话然后朗读 Match A with B to make up dialogues and read the dialogues aloud

| A | B |
|---|---|
| 我有点儿不舒服。 | 你最好请个小时工帮你收拾收拾。 |
| 我起床后脖子疼得很。 | 你最好早点儿睡。 |
| 我咳嗽得厉害。 | 你最好去医院看看。 |
| 来这儿以后，我越来越胖了。 | 最好让大夫给你按摩按摩。 |
| 我晚上十一点多才睡。 | 你最好少吃肉。 |
| 我的屋子太乱了。 | 你最好别抽烟。 |

（提示：生词请查阅各类词典。）

(Tip: For new words, please refer to various dictionaries.)

（六）根据实际情况回答问题 Answer the questions according to the actual situations

1. 你住学校宿舍还是在校外租房住？
2. 你的房间干净整齐吗？
3. 你的房间是自己收拾吗？
4. 你房间的墙上有什么？
5. 走进你的房间，感觉怎么样？
6. 说说你房间里的情况。

（七）跟同学一起练习下列会话 Practice the following conversation with your classmates

A：明天你有什么安排？
B：明天我想去博物馆看看，一起去吧。
A：参观博物馆要多长时间？
B：大约得两个小时。
A：博物馆离我们学校远吗？
B：不远。咱们最好骑车去。

（八）和同学一起表演课文 Act out the text with your classmates

（九）读后说 Read the passage and say it

　　我比较懒，不怎么收拾自己的房间，所以朋友说我的房间常常乱得像狗屋一样。上星期，我感冒了，病得很厉害。林老师来看我，她看我屋子乱七八糟的，都没法儿进屋了，就对我说："最好请个小时工帮你收拾收拾。"我给家政服务公司打了个电话，他们很快就派了一个小时工来，一星期来一次，一次一个小时。你们看，现在我的房间收拾得又干净又整齐，墙上挂着山水画，窗台上还摆着一盆花儿，整个房间布置得很漂亮。在这干净整齐的房间里学习和休息，太舒服了！

（十）怎么表达 How to express

> jiànyì
> 建议　making suggestions

　Nǐ zuìhǎo bié nàyàng zuò.
1. 你最好别那样做。
　You'd better not do that.

　Nín zuìhǎo qù yīyuàn kànkan.
2. 您最好去医院看看。
　You'd better go to see a doctor.

　Nǐ zuìhǎo bǎ yān jiè le.
3. 你最好把烟戒了。
　You'd better give up smoking.

(十一) 朗读中国经典诗词，请注意语音语调 Read aloud the classic Chinese poem and pay attention to the pronunciation and intonation

Yuánrì
元日

[Sòng] Wáng Ānshí
［宋］ 王 安石（1021—1086）

Bàozhú shēng zhōng yí suì chú, chūnfēng sòng nuǎn rù túsū.
爆竹 声 中 一 岁 除，春风 送 暖 入 屠苏。

Qiān mén wàn hù tóngtóng rì, zǒng bǎ xīn táo huàn jiù fú.
千 门 万 户 瞳瞳 日，总 把 新 桃 换 旧 符。

(十二) 请欣赏下列著名的词句 Please enjoy the following famous saying

Zhǐyào gōngfu shēn, tiě chǔ móchéng zhēn.
只要 功夫 深，铁 杵 磨成 针。

Constant grinding turns an iron rod into a needle.

# 第三十二课 今天我们从这条小路爬上去
Dì-sānshíèr kè　Jīntiān wǒmen cóng zhè tiáo xiǎo lù pá shangqu

Lesson 32　Today we'll take this path up

## 一 课文 Text

### （一）今天我们从这条小路爬上去

丹尼斯：今天 从 哪条 路 上去？
Dānnísī: Jīntiān cóng nǎ tiáo lù shàngqu?

李大同：今天我们 从 这条 小路爬上去，请 大家检查 一下 背包，要 注意 安全， 出发吧。
Lǐ Dàtóng: Jīntiān wǒmen cóng zhè tiáo xiǎo lù pá shangqu, qǐng dàjiā jiǎnchá yíxià bēibāo, yào zhùyì ānquán, chūfā ba.

丹尼斯：这儿离 山顶 有 多 远？ 从 这儿爬上去 要多 长 时间？
Dānnísī: Zhèr lí shāndǐng yǒu duō yuǎn? Cóng zhèr pá shangqu yào duō cháng shíjiān?

李大同：我也没有 从 这 条 小路爬上去 过，大概要 两个 多 小时吧。现在八点一刻，十点多 能 爬到 山顶。在 山 上 休息半个小时，再走下来。
Lǐ Dàtóng: Wǒ yě méiyǒu cóng zhè tiáo xiǎo lù pá shangqu guò, dàgài yào liǎng gè duō xiǎoshí ba. Xiànzài bā diǎn yí kè, shí diǎn duō néng pádào shāndǐng. Zài shān shang xiūxi bàn gè xiǎoshí, zài zǒu xialai.

丹尼斯：（一边拍照一边说）这一路的 风景 真 美 呀！
Dānnísī: Zhè yílù de fēngjǐng zhēn měi ya!

李大同：别 光 顾着拍照 了，快点儿爬上去 吧。
Lǐ Dàtóng: Bié guāng gùzhe pāi zhào le, kuài diǎnr pá shangqu ba.

丹尼斯：好的。我们爬了多 长 时间了？
Dānnísī: Hǎo de. Wǒmen pále duō cháng shíjiān le?

Lǐ Dàtóng: Yǐjīng pále liǎng gè duō zhōngtóu le.
李 大同：已经 爬了 两 个 多 钟头 了。

Dānnísī: Kuài dào shāndǐng le ba?
丹尼斯：快 到 山顶 了吧？

Lǐ Dàtóng: Mǎshàng jiù dào shāndǐng le.
李 大同：马上 就 到 山顶 了。

---

**Today we'll take this path up**

Dennis: Which way are we going up the hill today?

Li Datong: Today we'll take this path up. Please check your backpacks and be careful. Let's go.

Dennis: How far is it from here to the top of the mountain? How long will it take to climb up?

Li Datong: I have never taken this path either. It takes about two hours to climb up the mountain. It's a quarter past eight, and we can get to the top of the mountain by ten. We will rest on the mountain for half an hour, and then walk down the hill again.

Dennis: (Taking photos) The scenery is so beautiful.

Li Datong: Don't just take pictures. Climb up quickly.

Dennis: OK. How long have we been climbing?

Li Datong: We have been climbing for more than two hours.

Dennis: Are we near the top of the mountain?

Li Datong: We'll get to the top of the mountain soon.

## （二）终于爬上来了

Dānnísī: À, zhōngyú pá shanglai le, mǎn shān de hóngyè, zhēn hǎokàn.
丹尼斯：啊，终于 爬 上 来 了，满 山 的 红叶，真 好看。

Lǐ Dàtóng: Cóng zhèlǐ kàn xiaqu, shān xià de fēngjǐng yìlǎn-wúyú. Dānnísī,
李 大同：从 这里 看 下去，山 下 的 风景 一览无余。丹尼斯，
nǐ lèi bu lèi?
你 累不累？

Dānnísī: Yǒudiǎnr lèi.
丹尼斯：有点儿累。

Lǐ Dàtóng: Lèile jiù dào xiūxishì qù xiūxi yíhuìr. Sānshí fēnzhōng hòu, wǒ-
李 大同：累了就 到 休息室去 休息 一会儿。三十 分钟 后，我
men zài zǒu xiaqu.
们 再 走 下去。

Dānnísī: Wǒ búyòng xiūxi. Zhèxiē měijǐng wǒ dōu yào pāi xialai, fādào péng-
丹尼斯：我 不 用 休息。这些 美景 我 都 要 拍 下来，发到 朋

youquān li qù.
友圏 里去。

Lǐ Dàtóng: Nǐ jiù hǎohāor pāi ba, zhèlǐ chùchù jiē jǐng. Nàbiān yǒu
李 大同： 你就好好儿 拍 吧，这里 处处 皆 景。（对大家）那边 有

yì jiān xiūxishì, lǐbian yǒu wèishēngjiān, shéi xūyào kěyǐ qù fāngbiàn
一间 休息室，里边 有 卫生间，谁 需要 可以 去 方便

fāngbiàn.
方便。

Dàjiā: Zhīdào le, xièxie nǐ!
大家： 知道 了，谢谢 你！

Lǐ Dàtóng: Dānnísī, nǐ kuài guòlai, zhèr de fēngjǐng měijí le!
李 大同： 丹尼斯，你 快 过来，这儿的 风景 美极了！

Dānnísī: Hǎo. Wǒ mǎshàng jiù guòqu.
丹尼斯： 好。我 马上 就 过去。

**We are finally on top of the mountain**

Dennis: Ah, we are finally on top of the mountain. The red leaves are all over the mountain, so beautiful.

Li Datong: From here, the view of the mountain below is unobstructed. Dennis, are you tired?

Dennis: A little.

Li Datong: If you are tired, go to the lounge to have a rest. Thirty minutes later, we'll start to walk down the hill.

Dennis: I don't need a rest. I'm going to take pictures of all these beautiful places and post them on my WeChat Moments.

Li Datong: Take as many as you like. There are beautiful views everywhere. (To everyone) There is a lounge over there. There is a toilet in it. If anyone needs it, go to use it.

Everyone: OK. Thank you.

Li Datong: Dennis, come over here. The scenery here is so beautiful.

Dennis: Good. I'll be right there.

## （三）坚持就是胜利

Xīngqīliù nǐ qù nǎr le?
A: 星期六 你 去 哪儿 了？

Wǒ pá shān qù le.
B: 我 爬 山 去 了。

Nǐ shì yí gè rén qù de ma?
A: 你是一个 人 去 的 吗？

# 第三十二课 Lesson 32

B: 不是。我跟学校登山队一起去的。
Bú shì. Wǒ gēn xuéxiào dēngshānduì yìqǐ qù de.

A: 你们是怎么去的?
Nǐmen shì zěnme qù de?

B: 骑自行车去的。
Qí zìxíngchē qù de.

A: 你爬上去了吗?
Nǐ pá shangqu le ma?

B: 当然爬上去了。
Dāngrán pá shangqu le.

A: 爬了多长时间?
Pále duō cháng shíjiān?

B: 爬上去用了两个多小时,在山顶休息了半个钟头,走下来才用了不到两个小时,上去下来一共用了差不多五个小时。
Pá shangqu yòngle liǎng gè duō xiǎoshí, zài shāndǐng xiūxile bàn gè zhōngtóu, zǒu xialai cái yòngle bú dào liǎng gè xiǎoshí, shàngqu xiàlai yígòng yòngle chàbuduō wǔ gè xiǎoshí.

A: 什么时候回来的?
Shénme shíhou huílai de?

B: 回到学校都快两点了。
Huídào xuéxiào dōu kuài liǎng diǎn le.

A: 我真佩服你,能一直坚持去爬山。
Wǒ zhēn pèifu nǐ, néng yìzhí jiānchí qù pá shān.

B: 我是在锻炼自己的意志。坚持就是胜利嘛。
Wǒ shì zài duànliàn zìjǐ de yìzhì. Jiānchí jiù shì shènglì ma.

---

**Perseverance means victory**

A: Where did you go on Saturday?

B: I went mountain climbing.

A: Did you go there alone?

B: No, I didn't. I went with the school mountaineering team.

A: How did you get there?

B: We went there by bike.

A: Have you climbed to the top of the mountain?

B: Of course I did.

A: How long did it take?

B: It took us more than two hours to climb up the mountain, and we took a half-hour rest on the top. It took less than two hours to walk down the mountain. We spent about five hours altogether climbing up and down.

A: When did you get back?

B: It was almost two o'clock when we got back to school.

A: I really admire you for your perseverance in mountain climbing.

B: I'm exercising my willpower. Perseverance means victory.

## 二 生词 New Words

| | | | | |
|---|---|---|---|---|
| 1 | 上去 | shàngqu | 动 | to go up |
| | 上来 | shànglai | 动 | to come up |
| | 下来 | xiàlai | 动 | to come down |
| | 下去 | xiàqu | 动 | to go down |
| 2 | 检查 | jiǎnchá | 动 | to examine; to check |
| 3 | 背包 | bēibāo | 名 | backpack |
| 4 | 安全 | ānquán | 形 | safe |
| 5 | 山顶 | shāndǐng | 名 | mountaintop |
| 6 | 休息 | xiūxi | 动 | to have (or take) a rest; to rest |
| 7 | 钟头 | zhōngtóu | 名 | hour |
| 8 | 一边 | yìbiān | 副 | at the same time |
| 9 | 风景 | fēngjǐng | 名 | view; scenery |
| 10 | 光 | guāng | 副 | only |
| 11 | 顾 | gù | 动 | to attend to; to pay attention to |
| 12 | 终于 | zhōngyú | 副 | at last; finally |
| 13 | 红叶 | hóngyè | 名 | red autumnal leaf |
| 14 | 好看 | hǎokàn | 形 | beautiful; good-looking |

| 15 | 一览无余 | yìlǎn-wúyú | | to take in everything at a glance |
| 16 | 休息室 | xiūxishì | 名 | lounge; lobby |
| 17 | 一会儿 | yíhuìr | | a little while |
| 18 | 美景 | měijǐng | 名 | fine view; beautiful scenery |
| 19 | 朋友圈 | péngyouquān | 名 | WeChat Moments |
| 20 | 处处 | chùchù | 副 | everywhere |
| 21 | 皆 | jiē | 副 | all; each and every |
| 22 | 方便 | fāngbiàn | 动 | to go to the lavatory |
| 23 | 过来 | guòlai | 动 | to come over here |
| | 过去 | guòqu | 动 | to go over there |
| 24 | 极 | jí | 副 | extremely |
| 25 | 胜利 | shènglì | 动 | to win a victory; to triumph |
| 26 | 佩服 | pèifu | 动 | to admire |
| 27 | 意志 | yìzhì | 名 | willpower |

## 三 注释 Notes

### (一) 复合趋向补语 Compound complements of direction

趋向动词"上、下、进、出、回、过、起"加上"来"或"去",放在另一动词后面做补语,叫复合趋向补语,表示动作的趋向。常用的复合趋向补语如下表:

When a directional verb such as "上", "下", "进", "出", "回", "过" and "起" is followed by "来" or "去" and placed after another verb to function as a complement, it is called a compound complement of direction, indicating the direction of an action. The frequently-used ones are listed as follows:

|   | 上 | 下 | 进 | 出 | 回 | 过 | 起 |
|---|---|---|---|---|---|---|---|
| 来 | 上来 | 下来 | 进来 | 出来 | 回来 | 过来 | 起来 |
| 去 | 上去 | 下去 | 进去 | 出去 | 回去 | 过去 |   |

例如：

For example:

1. 今天我们从这条小路爬上去。（说话人在下边）
2. 在山上休息半个钟头，再走下来。（说话人在下边）
3. 终于爬上来了。（说话人在上边）
4. 三十分钟后，再走下去。（说话人在上边）

（二）丹尼斯一边拍照一边说。

副词"一边"用在动词前，表示两种或两种以上的动作同时进行。例如：

The adverb "一边" is used before a verb to indicate that two or more actions are proceeding at the same time. For example:

1. 我们一边走一边聊吧。
2. 我一边听老师讲，一边做笔记。
   不能说：*我一边听老师讲一边不懂。
3. 她们一边唱一边跳。

（三）快到山顶了吧？马上就到山顶了。

汉语用"快……了""要……了""快要……了""就要……了"表示动作或情况即将发生。例如：

In Chinese, "快……了", "要……了", "快要……了" or "就要……了" is used to indicate that something is about to happen. For example:

1. 下个星期就要考试了。
2. 新年快要到了。也可以说：新年就要到了。

注意：句中有表示具体时间的词语做状语时，不能用"快要……了"。例如：

Note: "快要……了" is not used if a sentence contains an adverbial which is a specific time. For example:

不能说：*一月十号快要放寒假了。

可以说：一月十号就要放寒假了。

（四）这些美景我都要拍下来。

句中"拍下来"是趋向补语的引申用法，表示动作使美景固定在手机里了。

In this sentence, "拍下来" is an extended use of the complement of direction, indicating that the action makes the fine view fixed on the phone.

（五）里边有卫生间，谁需要可以去方便方便。

句中"方便方便"是大小便的委婉说法。

"方便方便" is a euphemism for urination and defecation.

## 四　练习 Exercises

（一）朗读下列发音相近的词语 Read aloud the following words and expressions with similar pronunciation

| zhùyì | zhǔyi | ānquán | ānjiǎn |
| 注意 | 主意 | 安全 | 安检 |

| zhōngyú | zhōngyǔ | chùchù | chūchù |
| 终于 | 中雨 | 处处 | 出处 |

| xūyào | xīyào | fāngbiàn | fāngmiàn |
| 需要 | 西药 | 方便 | 方面 |

（二）替换并朗读 Replace and read aloud

1. 你是<u>走着</u>去的吗？

坐地铁　坐出租车
跟朋友一起　昨天

2. A：你是怎么去的？
   B：我是<u>一个人去</u>的。

   骑车　　打的　　坐地铁
   跟登山队一起
   跟朋友一起

3. A：用了多长时间？
   B：用了<u>两个多小时</u>。

   一个小时　半个小时　一刻钟
   两天　　　两年　　　四年

4. A：你什么时候回来的？
   B：我是<u>下午回来</u>的。

   昨天　　前天　　上星期
   上个月　去年

5. 这儿的风景美极了，我要拍<u>下来</u>。

   这支钢琴曲　　好听　　　录
   这篇文章　　　棒　　　　下载
   这首诗　　　　好　　　　背
   这个故事　　　有意思　　记

（提示：生词请查阅各类词典。）

(Tip: For new words, please refer to various dictionaries.)

（三）选词填空并朗读下列句子 Choose the appropriate words to fill in the blanks and read aloud the following sentences

再　下来　离　方便　去　从　到　看

1. 今天我们从这条小路爬上_____，请大家检查一下背包，要注意安全，出发吧。

2. 这儿_____山顶有多远？从这儿爬上去得多长时间？

3. 我也没有_____这条小路爬上去过，大概要两个多小时。

4. 现在八点一刻，十点多能爬到山顶。在山上休息半个小时，_____走下来。

5. 从这里_____下去，山下的风景一览无余。

6. 累了就_____休息室去休息一会儿。三十分钟后，我们再走下去。

7. 这些美景我要都拍_____，发到朋友圈里去。

8. 休息室里边有卫生间，谁需要可以去方便_____。

真　锻炼　跟　骑　了　上去

1. A：星期六你到哪儿去_____？
   B：我爬山去了。

2. A：你是一个人去的吗？
   B：我是_____学校登山队一起去的。

3. A：你们是怎么去的？
   B：我们是_____自行车去的。

4. A：你爬到山顶上去了吗？
   B：当然爬_____了。

5. 我_____佩服你，能坚持爬山。

6. 我是在_____自己的意志，坚持就是胜利嘛。

（四）说话人在哪儿 Where is the speaker

1. 今天我们要从这条小路爬上山去。　　（山上　山下）
   我们终于爬上山来了。　　　　　　　（山上　山下）
   我们现在要走下山去。　　　　　　　（山上　山下）
   我们走下山来了。　　　　　　　　　（山上　山下）

2. 他走进教室去了。　　　　　　　　　（教室里　教室外）
   他走出教室来了。　　　　　　　　　（教室里　教室外）
   他走进教室来了。　　　　　　　　　（教室里　教室外）
   他走出教室去了。　　　　　　　　　（教室里　教室外）

3. 他骑回公寓楼去了。　　　　　　　　　　（公寓楼　别的地方）
   他骑回公寓楼来了。　　　　　　　　　　（公寓楼　别的地方）
   她走过小桥去了。　　　　　　　　　　　（她前面　她后面）
   她走过小桥来了。　　　　　　　　　　　（她前面　她后面）

（五）完成下列会话并大声朗读 Complete the following conversations and read them aloud

1. A：今天我们怎么上去？
   B：＿＿＿＿＿＿＿＿＿＿＿＿＿＿＿＿＿＿＿爬上去。
2. A：从小路爬上去要多长时间？
   B：大概要＿＿＿＿＿＿＿＿＿＿＿＿＿＿＿＿。
3. A：累了你就休息一会儿吧。
   B：不用，＿＿＿＿＿＿＿＿＿＿＿＿＿＿，发到朋友圈里去。
4. A：你昨天是怎么去的？
   B：＿＿＿＿＿＿＿＿＿＿＿＿＿＿＿＿＿＿＿＿。
5. A：你一个人去的还是跟朋友一起去的？
   B：＿＿＿＿＿＿＿＿＿＿＿＿＿＿＿＿＿＿＿。
6. A：你爬到山顶上了吗？
   B：我当然＿＿＿＿＿＿＿＿＿＿＿＿＿＿＿＿。

（六）你是 A，请你向 B 提问 Supposing you are A, ask B questions

A：＿＿＿＿＿＿＿＿＿＿＿＿＿＿＿＿？
B：我最喜欢的运动是爬山。
A：＿＿＿＿＿＿＿＿＿＿＿＿＿＿＿＿？
B：来中国以后，我也坚持下来了。
A：＿＿＿＿＿＿＿＿＿＿＿＿＿＿＿＿？
B：一星期去爬一次。
A：＿＿＿＿＿＿＿＿＿＿＿＿＿＿＿＿？
B：不是，跟学校登山队一起去。
A：＿＿＿＿＿＿＿＿＿＿＿＿＿＿＿＿？
B：来回要半天时间。

A: _____？
B: 来了快一年了，我没有生过病。

（七）请用"快……了""要……了""就要……了""快要……了"说一个句子。
Please say a sentence using "快……了", "要……了", "就要……了", or "快要……了"

例如：7月10日放暑假，今天6月30日了。→要/快/快要/就要放暑假了。

1. 圣诞节是12月25日，今天是12月20日。
    → _____
2. 新年是1月1日，今天是12月26日。
    → _____
3. 我的生日是1月16号，今天是1月10号。
    → _____
4. 他准备7月15号回国，今天是7月11号。
    → _____
5. 我爸爸准备8月20号来中国旅行，今天是8月15号。
    → _____
6. 我哥哥10月5日结婚，今天是9月30日。
    → _____

（八）根据实际情况回答问题 Answer the questions according to the actual situations
1. 你爬过山吗？
2. 你喜欢爬山吗？
3. 你来中国以后经常锻炼吗？
4. 你是怎么锻炼身体的？
5. 你每天锻炼多长时间？
6. 你有没有交到中国朋友？

（九）和同学一起表演课文 Act out the text with your classmates

（十）读后说 Read the passage and say it
昨天我又跟学校登山队爬山去了。这次我们走的是没走过的一条小路。小路不太好走，但是路两边的风景很美。我们爬了两个多小时才爬到山顶，站在山顶往下看，满山的红叶，漂亮极了。眼前的美景我都用手机拍了下来，发到了朋友圈里。

爬山是很好的运动，可以锻炼自己的意志。因为坚持锻炼，所以我的身体也非常好。

## （十一）怎么表达 How to express

> pèifu
> 佩服　admiration

Wǒ pèifu tā de yǒngqì.
1. 我 佩服 她 的 勇气。
I admire her courage.

Wǒ dǎ xīnyǎnr li pèifu tā.
2. 我 打心眼儿里佩服她。
I admire her from the bottom of my heart.

Tā zhēn nénggàn, wǒ bùjīn àn'àn de pèifu tā.
3. 她 真 能干，我 不禁 暗暗 地 佩服 她。
She is a crackerjack, and I cannot help secretly admiring her.

## （十二）朗读中国经典诗词，请注意语音语调 Read aloud the classic Chinese poem and pay attention to the pronunciation and intonation

Shān Xíng
**山　行**

[Táng] Dù Mù
［唐］杜 牧（803—853）

Yuǎn shàng hán shān shí jìng xié, bái yún shēng chù yǒu rénjiā.
远 上 寒 山 石 径 斜，白 云 生 处 有 人 家。

Tíng chē zuò ài fēng lín wǎn, shuāng yè hóng yú Èryuè huā.
停 车 坐 爱 枫 林 晚，霜 叶 红 于 二月 花。

## （十三）请欣赏下列著名的词句 Please enjoy the following famous saying

Yì fēn gēngyún, yì fēn shōuhuò.
一 分 耕耘，一 分 收获。
No pains, no gains.

# 词汇表   Vocabulary

**A**
| | | | | |
|---|---|---|---|---|
| 安全 | ānquán | 形 | safe | 32 |
| 按照 | ànzhào | 介 | according to | 31 |

**B**
| | | | | |
|---|---|---|---|---|
| 摆 | bǎi | 动 | to place; to put | 31 |
| 班 | bān | 名 | class | 21 |
| 办 | bàn | 动 | to do; to handle | 20 |
| 半 | bàn | 数 | half | 23 |
| 半天 | bàntiān | | half a day | 26 |
| 帮助 | bāngzhù | 动 | to help | 21 |
| 包 | bāo | 量、名 | bag; package; bundle | 28 |
| 饱 | bǎo | 形 | full | 27 |
| 背包 | bēibāo | 名 | backpack | 32 |
| 本 | běn | 量、名 | *a measure word for books*; book; notebook | 29 |
| 必须 | bìxū | 副 | must | 22 |
| 变 | biàn | 动 | to change | 31 |
| 表 | biǎo | 名 | form | 20 |
| 别的 | biéde | 代 | other | 20 |
| 病 | bìng | 动、名 | to fall ill; illness | 31 |
| 不但 | búdàn | 连 | not only | 30 |
| 不过 | búguò | 连 | but; however | 22 |
| 不见不散 | bú jiàn bú sàn | | (let's) not leave without seeing each other (said when making an appointment) | 29 |
| 不管 | bùguǎn | 连 | no matter (what, how, etc.) | 22 |
| 不好意思 | bù hǎoyìsi | | embarrassed; awkward | 22 |

| | | | | |
|---|---|---|---|---|
| 不同 | bù tóng | | different | 30 |
| 不一定 | bù yídìng | | not necessarily | 29 |
| 布置 | bùzhì | 动 | to fix up; to arrange | 31 |
| 步 | bù | 名 | step; pace | 26 |
| **C** 菜 | cài | 名 | dishes; greens | 27 |
| 参加 | cānjiā | 动 | to join; to participate | 26 |
| 惭愧 | cánkuì | 形 | ashamed | 22 |
| 操场 | cāochǎng | 名 | playground | 26 |
| 草地 | cǎodì | 名 | lawn; ground covered with grass | 30 |
| 册 | cè | 名 | book; volume | 29 |
| 差不多 | chàbuduō | 副、形 | almost; about | 29 |
| 长 | cháng | 形 | long | 22 |
| 长跑 | chángpǎo | 名 | long-distance running | 26 |
| 超市 | chāoshì | 名 | supermarket | 28 |
| 成 | chéng | 动 | to become | 31 |
| 成才 | chéngcái | 动 | to become a useful person | 22 |
| 充电 | chōng diàn | 动 | to charge (a battery, etc.) | 25 |
| 充满 | chōngmǎn | 动 | to be full of | 30 |
| 抽空儿 | chōu kòngr | 动 | to find time | 29 |
| 出发 | chūfā | 动 | to start off; to depart | 26 |
| 出站 | chū zhàn | | to get out of the station | 29 |
| 处处 | chùchù | 副 | everywhere | 32 |
| 穿 | chuān | 动 | to wear | 19 |
| 窗台 | chuāngtái | 名 | windowsill | 31 |
| 词典 | cídiǎn | 名 | dictionary | 29 |
| 次 | cì | 量 | (*a measure word for repeated occurrences or events likely to be repeated*) time(s) | 20 |
| 聪明 | cōngmíng | 形 | clever; smart | 24 |
| 从来 | cónglái | 副 | (*usu. used with a negative*) from the past till the present; always | 29 |

| | | | | |
|---|---|---|---|---|
| 存折 | cúnzhé | 名 | bankbook | 20 |
| 错 | cuò | 形 | bad; poor (used in the negative: 不错 not bad) | 27 |

**D**

| | | | | |
|---|---|---|---|---|
| 打 | dǎ | 动 | to play | 24 |
| 大概 | dàgài | 副 | probably | 19 |
| 大量 | dàliàng | 形 | a large number of | 22 |
| 大学 | dàxué | 名 | university; college | 17 |
| 带 | dài | 动 | to take; to bring | 19 |
| 待 | dài | 动 | to treat; to deal with | 17 |
| 戴 | dài | 动 | to adorn; to wear (accessories) | 24 |
| 但是 | dànshì | 连 | but; yet | 30 |
| 当 | dāng | 动 | to be; to work as | 18 |
| 导航仪 | dǎohángyí | 名 | navigator | 25 |
| 到 | dào | 动 | to come/go to | 17 |
| 到处 | dàochù | 副 | everywhere | 30 |
| 地 | de | 助 | *used after an adjective or phrase to form an adverbial adjunct before a verb* | 21 |
| 登山 | dēng shān | 动 | to climb a mountain | 26 |
| 登山队 | dēngshānduì | 名 | mountaineering team | 26 |
| 等 | děng | 动 | to wait | 27 |
| 低 | dī | 形 | low | 22 |
| 地方 | dìfang | 名 | place | 30 |
| 地铁 | dìtiě | 名 | subway; metro | 29 |
| 地图 | dìtú | 名 | map | 29 |
| 第 | dì | 词头 | *used before numerals to form ordinal numbers* 第三食堂 | 27 |
| 点（钟） | diǎn(zhōng) | 量 | o'clock | 23 |
| 电动车 | diàndòngchē | 名 | electric bicycle | 19 |
| 电脑 | diànnǎo | 名 | computer | 25 |

| | 电视机 | diànshìjī | 名 | television | 25 |
|---|---|---|---|---|---|
| | 东西 | dōngxi | 名 | thing; stuff | 28 |
| | 都 | dōu | 副 | already | 24 |
| | 堵车 | dǔ chē | 动 | traffic jam | 29 |
| | 锻炼 | duànliàn | 动 | to take exercise; to have physical training | 26 |
| | 对 | duì | 动 | with regard to; concerning; to | 17 |
| | 多 | duō | 代 | how; what | 22 |
| | 多 | duō | 副 | how; to what extent | 23 |
| **E** | 而且 | érqiě | 连 | but also | 30 |
| **F** | 饭 | fàn | 名 | meal; food | 27 |
| | 方便 | fāngbiàn | 动 | to go to the lavatory | 32 |
| | 房东 | fángdōng | 名 | owner of a house; landlord/landlady | 17 |
| | 房间 | fángjiān | 名 | room | 17 |
| | 放心 | fàng xīn | 动 | to be at ease; to feel relieved | 21 |
| | 非常 | fēicháng | 副 | very | 17 |
| | 分钟 | fēnzhōng | 量 | minute | 19 |
| | 风 | fēng | 名 | wind | 26 |
| | 风景 | fēngjǐng | 名 | view; scenery | 32 |
| | 夫妇 | fūfù | 名 | husband and wife | 17 |
| | 肤色 | fūsè | 名 | skin color | 30 |
| | 服务 | fúwù | 动 | to serve | 31 |
| | 幅 | fú | 量 | *a measure word for paintings* | 31 |
| | 付费 | fùfèi | 动 | to pay | 31 |
| **G** | 该 | gāi | 助动 | should; ought to | 24 |
| | 干净 | gānjìng | 形 | clean | 31 |
| | 感觉 | gǎnjué | 动 | to feel | 29 |
| | 感冒 | gǎnmào | 动 | to have a cold; to catch a cold | 31 |
| | 干 | gàn | 动 | to do | 25 |

| | | | | |
|---|---|---|---|---|
| 刚才 | gāngcái | 名 | just now | 26 |
| 告诉 | gàosu | 动 | to tell | 19 |
| 隔壁 | gébì | 名 | next door | 31 |
| 各种各样 | gèzhǒng-gèyàng | | all kinds of | 28 |
| 更 | gèng | 副 | even more | 21 |
| 工人 | gōngrén | 名 | worker | 31 |
| 公司 | gōngsī | 名 | company; firm | 22 |
| 公寓 | gōngyù | 名 | apartment | 17 |
| 功课 | gōngkè | 名 | homework; lesson; schoolwork | 22 |
| 功能 | gōngnéng | 名 | function | 25 |
| 狗屋 | gǒuwū | 名 | doghouse | 31 |
| 顾 | gù | 动 | to attend to; to pay attention to | 32 |
| 刮 | guā | 动 | (of wind) to blow | 26 |
| 挂 | guà | 动 | to hang | 31 |
| 关爱 | guān'ài | 动 | to care and love | 21 |
| 关心 | guānxīn | 动 | to care about | 21 |
| 关照 | guānzhào | 动 | to look after | 18 |
| 光 | guāng | 副 | only | 32 |
| 逛 | guàng | 动 | to stroll; to roam | 28 |
| 规模 | guīmó | 名 | scale | 29 |
| 国家 | guójiā | 名 | country | 21 |
| 果酱 | guǒjiàng | 名 | jam | 28 |
| 过 | guò | 动 | to spend (time); to pass (time) | 21 |
| 过奖 | guòjiǎng | 动 | to flatter (sb.) | 22 |
| 过来 | guòlai | 动 | to come over here | 32 |
| 过去 | guòqu | 动 | to go over there | 32 |

**H**

| | | | | |
|---|---|---|---|---|
| 还是 | háishi | 副 | still; yet | 19 |
| 还是 | háishi | 副 | (*expressing hope*) had better | 23 |
| 汗 | hàn | 名 | sweat | 26 |

| | | | | | |
|---|---|---|---|---|---|
| 好看 | hǎokàn | 形 | beautiful; good-looking | | 32 |
| 好玩儿 | hǎowánr | 形 | amusing; fun | | 24 |
| 好像 | hǎoxiàng | 动 | to seem; as if | | 30 |
| 好用 | hǎoyòng | 形 | easy to use | | 25 |
| 合住 | hé zhù | | to live together; to share an apartment | | 17 |
| 和谐 | héxié | 形 | harmonious | | 21 |
| 盒 | hé | 量、名 | box | | 28 |
| 嘿 | hēi | 叹 | hi; hey | | 26 |
| 红叶 | hóngyè | 名 | red autumnal leaf | | 32 |
| 湖 | hú | 名 | lake | | 30 |
| 护照 | hùzhào | 名 | passport | | 20 |
| 花生 | huāshēng | 名 | peanut | | 28 |
| 花园 | huāyuán | 名 | garden | | 30 |
| 化妆 | huà zhuāng | 动 | to put on make-up | | 24 |
| 坏 | huài | 形 | bad; broken | | 28 |
| 回 | huí | 动 | to return; to come/go back | | 26 |
| 回 | huí | 量 | (*indicating frequency of occurrence*) time | | 31 |
| 回来 | huílai | 动 | to return; to come back | | 26 |
| 活 | huó | 动 | to live | | 25 |
| 活力 | huólì | 名 | vigor | | 30 |
| 活期 | huóqī | 形 | due on demand | | 20 |
| 或者 | huòzhě | 连 | or | | 19 |
| **J** 极 | jí | 副 | extremely | | 32 |
| 计算机 | jìsuànjī | 名 | computer | | 18 |
| 计算器 | jìsuànqì | 名 | calculator | | 25 |
| 记得 | jìde | 动 | to remember | | 31 |
| 既 | jì | 副 | used correlatively with adverb 也 yě, 又 yòu, *etc.*, to show two situations are available | | 21 |

| | | | | |
|---|---|---|---|---|
| 家庭 | jiātíng | 名 | family | 21 |
| 家政 | jiāzhèng | 名 | housekeeping; homemaking | 31 |
| 坚持 | jiānchí | 动 | to insist | 23 |
| 检查 | jiǎnchá | 动 | to examine; to check | 32 |
| 简直 | jiǎnzhí | 副 | simply | 25 |
| 见 | jiàn | 动 | to see; to meet with | 29 |
| 见识 | jiànshi | 名 | knowledge | 29 |
| 建议 | jiànyì | 动、名 | to suggest; suggestion | 31 |
| 健美操 | jiànměicāo | 名 | aerobics | 26 |
| 交通 | jiāotōng | 名 | transportation | 18 |
| 娇气 | jiāoqì | 形 | delicate; fragile | 24 |
| 教 | jiāo | 动 | to teach | 21 |
| 较 | jiào | 副 | relatively; rather; quite | 22 |
| 教室 | jiàoshì | 名 | classroom | 19 |
| 教授 | jiàoshòu | 名 | professor | 17 |
| 皆 | jiē | 副 | all; each and every | 32 |
| 结账 | jié zhàng | 动 | to settle accounts; to pay the bill | 28 |
| 姐妹 | jiěmèi | 名 | sister | 21 |
| 借 | jiè | 动 | to borrow | 22 |
| 今年 | jīnnián | 名 | this year | 18 |
| 进步 | jìnbù | 动 | to progress; to advance; to step forward | 22 |
| 精彩 | jīngcǎi | 形 | wonderful; brilliant; splendid | 25 |
| 旧 | jiù | 形 | old | 25 |
| 就 | jiù | 副 | only; merely; just | 31 |
| 就 | jiù | 副 | at once; right; away | 32 |

| | | | | |
|---|---|---|---|---|
| 开 | kāi | 动 | to open (an account in a bank) | 20 |
| 开通 | kāitōng | 动 | to open (a service) | 20 |
| 开玩笑 | kāi wánxiào | | to crack a joke; to make fun of | 31 |

| | | | | |
|---|---|---|---|---|
| 科学 | kēxué | 名 | science | 18 |
| 科学家 | kēxuéjiā | 名 | scientist | 18 |
| 可 | kě | 动 | to be worth (doing) | 17 |
| 可敬 | kějìng | 形 | worthy of respect; respectable | 17 |
| 可亲 | kěqīn | 形 | amiable; affable; genial | 17 |
| 刻 | kè | 量 | quarter | 24 |
| 刻 | kè | 动 | to sculpture; to engrave; to carve | 30 |
| 课外 | kèwài | 名 | after school; outside class | 22 |
| 空儿 | kòngr | 名 | free time | 17 |
| 哭 | kū | 动 | to cry; to weep | 24 |
| 快 | kuài | 形 | fast | 22 |
| 矿泉水 | kuàngquánshuǐ | 名 | mineral water | 27 |

**L**

| | | | | |
|---|---|---|---|---|
| 来回 | láihuí | 动 | to and fro | 26 |
| 来自 | láizì | 动 | to come from | 21 |
| 篮球 | lánqiú | 名 | basketball | 24 |
| 懒 | lǎn | 形 | lazy | 23 |
| 老人 | lǎorén | 名 | old person | 17 |
| 了 | le | 助 | used at the end of a sentence or a pause in the middle of a sentence to indicate a change or new situation | 26 |
| 了 | le | 助 | used after a verb or an adjective to indicate the completion of an action or a change | 27 |
| 离 | lí | 动 | to be away from | 19 |
| 里边 | lǐbian | 名 | inside; in | 19 |
| 理想 | lǐxiǎng | 名 | ideal; dream | 18 |
| 立 | lì | 动 | to set up; to stand | 30 |
| 厉害 | lìhai | 形 | serious; intense; terrible | 31 |
| 里 | •li | 名 | inside | 17 |
| 联系 | liánxì | 动 | to contact | 18 |

| | | | | | |
|---|---|---|---|---|---|
| | 脸 | liǎn | 名 | face | 23 |
| | 练功 | liàn gōng | 动 | to practice one's skill | 26 |
| | 了解 | liǎojiě | 动 | to understand; to know | 29 |
| | 绿 | lǜ | 形 | green | 30 |
| | 乱 | luàn | 形 | in a mess | 31 |
| | 乱七八糟 | luànqībāzāo | | in a mess | 31 |
| **M** | 麻烦 | máfan | 形、动 | troublesome; to bother | 25 |
| | 马路 | mǎlù | 名 | road | 19 |
| | 满 | mǎn | 形 | full; filled | 26 |
| | 满头大汗 | mǎn tóu dà hàn | | to be covered with sweat on one's head | 26 |
| | 毛笔 | máobǐ | 名 | writing brush | 28 |
| | 帽子 | màozi | 名 | cap; hat | 24 |
| | 没法儿 | méifǎr | 动 | cannot; to be impossible | 25 |
| | 美景 | měijǐng | 名 | fine view; beautiful scenery | 32 |
| | 门 | mén | 名 | door | 17 |
| | 门口儿 | ménkǒur | 名 | gate; entrance | 29 |
| | 梦想 | mèngxiǎng | 动、名 | dream | 30 |
| | 迷 | mí | 动 | to be fascinated by | 26 |
| | 密码 | mìmǎ | 名 | password | 20 |
| | 面 | miàn | 名 | noodles; flour | 27 |
| | 面 | miàn | 量 | *a measure word for flat things, such as walls, flags, mirrors, etc.* | 30 |
| | 明年 | míngnián | 名 | next year | 18 |
| | 墨汁 | mòzhī | 名 | prepared Chinese ink | 28 |
| | 目的 | mùdì | 名 | purpose; aim | 30 |
| **N** | 耐心 | nàixīn | 名、形 | patience; patient (with sth. or sb.) | 21 |
| | 男 | nán | 形 | man; male 男/女学生 boy/girl student | 18 |
| | 难怪 | nánguài | 动、副 | no wonder; understandable | 23 |

| | | | | | |
|---|---|---|---|---|---|
| | 内 | nèi | 名 | inside | 17 |
| | 能力 | nénglì | 名 | capacity; ability | 22 |
| | 牛肉面 | niúròumiàn | 名 | beef noodles | 27 |
| | 女 | nǚ | 形 | woman; female 女护士 female nurse | 18 |
| **P** | 爬 | pá | 动 | to climb | 26 |
| | 爬山 | pá shān | | to climb a mountain | 26 |
| | 拍照 | pāi zhào | 动 | to take a photo | 20 |
| | 跑 | pǎo | 动 | to run | 26 |
| | 跑步 | pǎo bù | 动 | to run | 26 |
| | 佩服 | pèifu | 动 | to admire | 32 |
| | 盆 | pén | 名 | pot | 31 |
| | 朋友圈 | péngyouquān | 名 | WeChat Moments | 32 |
| | 碰 | pèng | 动 | to meet by chance | 26 |
| | 啤酒 | píjiǔ | 名 | beer | 27 |
| | 漂亮 | piàoliang | 形 | pretty; beautiful | 24 |
| | 乒乓球 | pīngpāngqiú | 名 | ping-pong; table tennis | 24 |
| | 瓶 | píng | 量、名 | bottle | 28 |
| **Q** | 齐全 | qíquán | 形 | complete | 25 |
| | 骑 | qí | 动 | to ride | 19 |
| | 起床 | qǐ chuáng | 动 | to get up | 23 |
| | 气象台 | qìxiàngtái | 名 | meterological observatory | 25 |
| | 前 | qián | 名 | front | 19 |
| | 前边 | qiánbian | 名 | in front; ahead | 19 |
| | 墙 | qiáng | 名 | wall | 30 |
| | 桥 | qiáo | 名 | bridge | 30 |
| | 巧克力 | qiǎokèlì | 名 | chocolate | 28 |
| | 亲切 | qīnqiè | 形 | kind; cordial | 21 |
| | 清楚 | qīngchu | 动、形 | clear | 30 |
| | 请假 | qǐng jià | 动 | to ask for leave | 23 |

| | 圈儿 | quānr | 名、量 | circle; lap | 26 |
|---|---|---|---|---|---|
| **R** | 然后 | ránhòu | 连 | then; afterwards; after that | 18 |
| | 让 | ràng | 动 | to let; to allow | 22 |
| | 热闹 | rènao | 形 | lively; busy | 29 |
| | 热情 | rèqíng | 形 | enthusiastic; zealous; warm | 21 |
| | 人工 | réngōng | 形 | artificial | 18 |
| | 人工智能 | réngōng-zhìnéng | | Artificial Intelligence (AI) | 18 |
| | 人们 | rénmen | 名 | people | 30 |
| | 认真 | rènzhēn | 形 | earnest; careful | 21 |
| | 日历 | rìlì | 名 | calendar | 25 |
| **S** | 散 | sàn | 动 | to disperse; to separate | 29 |
| | 散步 | sàn bù | 动 | to take a walk | 30 |
| | 山 | shān | 名 | mountain | 26 |
| | 山顶 | shāndǐng | 名 | mountaintop | 32 |
| | 山水画 | shānshuǐhuà | 名 | landscape painting | 31 |
| | 商城 | shāngchéng | 名 | shopping mall; store | 29 |
| | 上 | shàng | 动 | *used as a complement after a verb* | 19 |
| | 上 | shàng | 动 | to go to (school, work, etc.) | 30 |
| | 上车 | shàng chē | | to get on the vehicle | 19 |
| | 上次 | shàng cì | | last time | 31 |
| | 上来 | shànglai | 动 | to come up | 32 |
| | 上面 | shàngmiàn | 名 | surface of sth. | 30 |
| | 上去 | shàngqu | 动 | to go up | 32 |
| | 上网 | shàng wǎng | 动 | to surf the Internet | 29 |
| | 社会 | shèhuì | 名 | society | 29 |
| | 生活 | shēnghuó | 名 | living; life | 30 |
| | 生命 | shēngmìng | 名 | life | 26 |
| | 胜利 | shènglì | 动 | to win a victory; to triumph | 32 |
| | 时候 | shíhou | 名 | (the duration of) time | 17 |

| | | | | |
|---|---|---|---|---|
| 时间 | shíjiān | 名 | time | 22 |
| 食堂 | shítáng | 名 | dining hall; canteen | 27 |
| 试 | shì | 动 | to try | 29 |
| 收 | shōu | 动 | to receive; to collect | 30 |
| 收到 | shōudào | 动 | to receive; to obtain | 30 |
| 收拾 | shōushi | 动 | to clear up; to put in order | 31 |
| 手机 | shǒujī | 名 | mobile phone; cell phone | 20 |
| 书 | shū | 名 | book | 22 |
| 书市 | shūshì | 名 | book fair; book market | 29 |
| 舒服 | shūfu | 形 | well; comfortable | 23 |
| 输入 | shūrù | 动 | to input | 20 |
| 输入密码 | shūrù mìmǎ | | to enter a password | 20 |
| 树 | shù | 名 | tree | 30 |
| 刷 | shuā | 动 | to brush | 23 |
| 刷卡 | shuā kǎ | 动 | to swipe a card | 28 |
| 水平 | shuǐpíng | 名 | level; standard | 22 |
| 睡懒觉 | shuì lǎnjiào | | to get up late; to sleep in | 23 |
| 睡觉 | shuì jiào | 动 | to sleep; to go to bed | 23 |
| 送 | sòng | 动 | to send; to deliver | 29 |
| 送货上门 | sòng huò shàng mén | | to deliver goods to one's door | 29 |
| 速度 | sùdù | 名 | speed | 25 |
| 虽然 | suīrán | 连 | though; although | 30 |
| 随时 | suíshí | 副 | at any time | 18 |
| 岁 | suì | 量 | year of age | 18 |
| 所以 | suǒyǐ | 连 | therefore; so | 28 |
|  台灯 | táidēng | 名 | table lamp | 28 |
| 太极拳 | tàijíquán | 名 | *taijiquan*, shadowboxing | 26 |
| 逃课 | táo kè | 动 | to skip class | 23 |
| 特别 | tèbié | 副、形 | especially; special | 21 |

| | | | | | |
|---|---|---|---|---|---|
| | 踢 | tī | 动 | to kick | 24 |
| | 替 | tì | 动 | for; in place of | 23 |
| | 填表 | tián biǎo | | to fill in a form | 20 |
| | 听说 | tīngshuō | 动 | to hear of; to hear about | 17 |
| | 同屋 | tóngwū | 名 | roommate | 18 |
| | 头 | tóu | 名 | head | 26 |
| | 图书馆 | túshūguǎn | 名 | library | 22 |
| | 腿 | tuǐ | 名 | leg | 19 |
| | 退休 | tuìxiū | 动 | to retire | 17 |
| **W** | 外 | wài | 名 | outside | 17 |
| | 完 | wán | 动 | to be finished; to be over | 26 |
| | 玩儿 | wánr | 动 | to play | 17 |
| | 碗 | wǎn | 名 | bowl | 27 |
| | 网购 | wǎnggòu | 动 | to shop online | 29 |
| | 网球 | wǎngqiú | 名 | tennis | 24 |
| | 往 | wǎng | 介 | to; towards | 19 |
| | 卫生间 | wèishēngjiān | 名 | bathroom; restroom; toilet | 23 |
| | 为了 | wèile | 介 | for; in order to | 30 |
| | 位 | wèi | 量 | *a polite measure word for people* | 17 |
| | 味道 | wèidào | 名 | taste | 27 |
| | 文化 | wénhuà | 名 | culture | 29 |
| | 屋子 | wūzi | 名 | room | 31 |
| | 无微不至 | wúwēi-búzhì | | meticulously | 21 |
| | 武术 | wǔshù | 名 | martial arts | 26 |
| **X** | 希望 | xīwàng | 动、名 | hope | 21 |
| | 习惯 | xíguàn | 动、名 | to get used to; habit | 30 |
| | 洗 | xǐ | 动 | to wash | 23 |
| | 洗澡 | xǐ zǎo | 动 | to take a bath | 23 |
| | 系 | xì | 名 | department | 18 |

| | | | | | |
|---|---|---|---|---|---|
| 下来 | xiàlai | 动 | to come down | 32 | |
| 下去 | xiàqu | 动 | to go down | 32 | |
| 先 | xiān | 副 | first | 18 | |
| 鲜花 | xiānhuā | 名 | (fresh) flower | 30 | |
| 羡慕 | xiànmù | 动 | to admire; to envy | 30 | |
| 相处 | xiāngchǔ | 动 | to get along with | 17 | |
| 相同 | xiāngtóng | 形 | same | 30 | |
| 小时 | xiǎoshí | 名 | hour | 31 | |
| 小时工 | xiǎoshígōng | 名 | hourly worker | 31 | |
| 校内 | xiào nèi | | on campus | 17 | |
| 校外 | xiào wài | | off campus | 17 | |
| 校园 | xiàoyuán | 名 | campus | 30 | |
| 笑 | xiào | 动 | to laugh; to smile | 24 | |
| 新 | xīn | 形 | new | 25 | |
| 信息 | xìnxī | 名 | information | 31 | |
| 幸运 | xìngyùn | 形 | lucky | 17 | |
| 兄弟 | xiōngdì | 名 | brother | 21 | |
| 休息 | xiūxi | 动 | to have (or take) a rest; to rest | 32 | |
| 休息室 | xiūxishì | 名 | lounge; lobby | 32 | |
| 需要 | xūyào | 动 | to need | 26 | |
| 宣纸 | xuānzhǐ | 名 | rice paper; *xuan* paper | 28 | |

**Y**

| | | | | | |
|---|---|---|---|---|---|
| 牙 | yá | 名 | tooth (pl. teeth) | 23 | |
| 眼镜 | yǎnjìng | 名 | glasses | 24 | |
| 要 | yào | 助动 | will; be going to | 18 | |
| 要 | yào | 动 | to order; to buy; to ask for | 27 | |
| 要是 | yàoshi | 连 | if; in case | 22 | |
| 业务 | yèwù | 名 | business | 20 | |
| 衣服 | yīfu | 名 | clothes | 24 | |
| 一定 | yídìng | 形 | certain; definite | 29 | |

| | | | | |
|---|---|---|---|---|
| 一会儿 | yíhuìr | | a little while | 32 |
| 一块儿 | yíkuàir | 副 | together | 27 |
| 一下子 | yíxiàzi | 副 | in a short while; suddenly | 31 |
| 一样 | yíyàng | 形 | the same; alike | 17 |
| 已经 | yǐjīng | 副 | already | 27 |
| 以后 | yǐhòu | 名 | afterwards | 18 |
| 一边 | yìbiān | 副 | at the same time | 32 |
| 一览无余 | yìlǎn-wúyú | | to take in everything at a glance | 32 |
| 一直 | yìzhí | 副 | all the time; straight | 19 |
| 意志 | yìzhì | 名 | willpower | 32 |
| 因为 | yīnwèi | 连 | because | 28 |
| 银行 | yínháng | 名 | bank | 19 |
| 银行卡 | yínhángkǎ | 名 | bank card | 20 |
| 应该 | yīnggāi | 助动 | should; ought to | 23 |
| 应有尽有 | yīngyǒu-jìnyǒu | | to have everything that one expects to find | 28 |
| 营业员 | yíngyèyuán | 名 | (bank) clerk | 20 |
| 游戏 | yóuxì | 名、动 | game; to play a game | 24 |
| 游泳 | yóu yǒng | 动 | to swim | 26 |
| 有时候 | yǒushíhou | 副 | sometimes | 23 |
| 又 | yòu | 副 | and also; as well as | 28 |
| 右边 | yòubian | 名 | right side | 19 |
| 愉快 | yúkuài | 形 | happy; cheerful | 21 |
| 雨 | yǔ | 名 | rain | 19 |
| 雨伞 | yǔsǎn | 名 | umbrella | 19 |
| 雨衣 | yǔyī | 名 | raincoat | 19 |
| 远 | yuǎn | 形 | far; distant | 19 |
| 阅览室 | yuèlǎnshì | 名 | reading room | 22 |
| 运动 | yùndòng | 名、动 | sports; to exercise | 26 |

## Z

| 再 | zài | 副 | once more; again | 27 |
| --- | --- | --- | --- | --- |
| 在 | zài | 副 | *indicating an action in progress* | 24 |
| 在于 | zàiyú | 动 | to lie in; to depend on | 26 |
| 糟糕 | zāogāo | 形 | bad; terrible | 24 |
| 早晨 | zǎochen | 名 | morning | 26 |
| 早饭 | zǎofàn | 名 | breakfast | 23 |
| 早上 | zǎoshang | 名 | morning | 23 |
| 张 | zhāng | 量 | (*a measure word for paper, drawings, etc.*) piece; sheet | 20 |
| 账户 | zhànghù | 名 | account | 20 |
| 照相机 | zhàoxiàngjī | 名 | camera | 25 |
| 这么 | zhème | 代 | so; such; like this | 19 |
| 着 | zhe | 助 | *indicating the continuation of an action or a state* | 24 |
| 争取 | zhēngqǔ | 动 | to strive for; to endeavor to | 22 |
| 整个 | zhěnggè | 形 | whole | 31 |
| 整齐 | zhěngqí | 形 | in good order; tidy | 31 |
| 正在 | zhèngzài | 副 | in the process of; in the course of | 24 |
| 支 | zhī | 量 | *a measure word for pens, pencils, etc.* | 28 |
| 支付 | zhīfù | 动 | to pay | 28 |
| 只是 | zhǐshì | 副 | only | 29 |
| 只要 | zhǐyào | 连 | as long as; if only | 26 |
| 指南针 | zhǐnánzhēn | 名 | compass | 25 |
| 智能 | zhìnéng | 名 | intelligence | 18 |
| 智能 | zhìnéng | 形 | intelligent; smart | 25 |
| 中医 | zhōngyī | 名 | traditional Chinese medicine | 18 |
| 终于 | zhōngyú | 副 | at last; finally | 32 |
| 钟表 | zhōngbiǎo | 名 | clock and watch | 25 |
| 钟头 | zhōngtóu | 名 | hour | 32 |
| 住 | zhù | 动 | to live (somewhere) | 17 |

| | | | | |
|---|---|---|---|---|
| 抓紧 | zhuājǐn | 动 | to firmly grasp; to lose no time | 22 |
| 仔细 | zǐxì | 形 | careful | 30 |
| 自己 | zìjǐ | 代 | oneself | 17 |
| 自我 | zìwǒ | 代 | self | 18 |
| 自学 | zìxué | 动 | to study on one's own | 22 |
| 总之 | zǒngzhī | 连 | in a word; all in all | 25 |
| 足球 | zúqiú | 名 | football; soccer | 24 |
| 组织 | zǔzhī | 动、名 | to organize; organization | 26 |
| 最 | zuì | 副 | most | 31 |
| 最好 | zuìhǎo | 副 | had better | 31 |
| 左边 | zuǒbian | 名 | left side | 19 |
| 座 | zuò | 名、量 | *a measure word for mountains, buildings, and other similar immovable objects* | 30 |

## 专名　Proper Nouns

| | | | |
|---|---|---|---|
| 阿里 | Ālǐ | Ali, a Tanzanian student | 18 |
| 艾和平 | Ài Hépíng | Ai Heping, a Kenyan student | 18 |
| 爱德华 | Àidéhuá | Edward | 18 |
| 安丽 | Ānlì | Anli, a German student | 17 |
| 常浩 | Cháng Hào | Chang Hao, a student | 19 |
| 德国 | Déguó | Germany | 18 |
| 韩国 | Hánguó | South Korea | 18 |
| 吉米 | Jímǐ | Jimmy | 25 |
| 加拿大 | Jiānádà | Canada | 18 |
| 肯尼亚 | Kěnníyà | Kenya | 18 |
| 李贤贞 | Lǐ Xiánzhēn | Li Xianzhen, a Korean student | 18 |
| 联合国 | Liánhéguó | the United Nations | 30 |
| 清华大学 | Qīnghuá Dàxué | Tsinghua University | 18 |
| 日本 | Rìběn | Japan | 18 |
| 山本幸子 | Shānběn Xìngzǐ | Sachiko Yamamoto, a Japanese student | 18 |
| 松山 | Sōngshān | Matsuyama, a Japanese student | 19 |
| 坦桑尼亚 | Tǎnsāngníyà | Tanzania | 18 |
| 王伟国 | Wáng Wěiguó | Wang Weiguo, a Chinese teacher | 18 |